SOCIAL LIFE
IN ENGLAND
THROUGH THE CENTURIES

BY

H. R. WILTON HALL

Library Curator, Hertfordshire County Museum;
Sub-Librarian, St. Alban's Cathedral ; Author of
"Hertfordshire: a Reading-book of the County"
&c.

HEALTH AND BEAUTY IN MODERN TOWN PLANNING.

A street in the Hampstead Garden Suburb, London, N.W.

PREFACE

In the course of the last ten or twelve years there has been a very marked development of interest in local history, and with it a desire not merely to "know more about the past" but a desire to appreciate intelligently the real value of those things, still to be seen, which speak of the gradual building up of the social life of the Nation, which rightly handled will play an important part in the work of reconstruction pressing upon us now, with its enormous difficulties and anxieties.

Much has been done in schools of all grades to utilize the material at hand—the things which can be seen in the locality—as an educational medium, opening out great possibilities for the development of curiosity, interest, personality, and power of initiative on the part of the children which, though it may not seem to yield any immediate results which can be appraised by examination methods on the lines of any "Syllabus", are "neither barren nor unfruitful".

Just now there are a number of schemes in the air for the institution of "Regional Survey" in schools, and a tendency amongst enthusiasts to get it put into school time-tables as a Syllabus Subject. However admirable the intention may be, and is, it is not as a Subject, but rather as a method in education, that its real value lies. "Regional Study" embraces so many subjects and they cannot be enterprised all at once, either by children or by anybody else.

This little book is intended to be suggestive, to stimulate interest and an intelligent curiosity, but it may serve as a foundation for conversational or more formal lessons and investigations under the teacher's direction, as his personal predilection, opportunities, taste, and judgment shall determine.

In the work of "Regional Study", where carried on with discrimination and with a commonsense apprehension of "relative values" it may be truly said:—

> " Nothing useless is, or low ;
>   Each thing in its place is best ;
>   And what seems but idle show,
>   Strengthens and supports the rest ".

H. R. W. H.

HERTFORDSHIRE COUNTY MUSEUM,
ST. ALBAN'S, *September, 1919.*

CONTENTS

CONTENTS

LIST OF PLATES

SOCIAL
LIFE IN ENGLAND

CHAPTER I

Introduction

A little boy, who had been born in a log-cabin in the backwoods of Canada, was taken by his father, when he was about eight years old, to the nearest settlement, for the first time in his life. The little fellow had never till then seen any other house than that in which he had been born, for the settlement was many miles away. "Father," he said, "what makes all the houses come together?"

Now that sounds a very strange and foolish question to ask; but it is by no means as foolish a question as it seems. Here, in England, there are towns and villages dotted about all over the country. Some of them are near the sea, on some big bay or inlet; others stand a little farther inland, on the banks of tidal rivers; others are far away from the sea, in sheltered valleys or on the sunny slopes of hills; some stand in the midst of broad fertile plains, while others are on the verge of bleak lonely moorlands. What has made all the houses in these towns and villages come together in these particular spots? There must be a reason in every case why a particular spot should have been chosen in the first instance.

In trying to find an answer to this question with reference to any town or village in our country we have to go back, far back, into the past. We may have to go back to ages long before there was any written history. As we go back step by step into the past we learn much of the people who have lived before us—of their ways and their doings, and of the part they played in the life and work of the country.

The little Canadian boy's question can be asked about every town and village in the land. There are no two places exactly alike; each one has its own history, which, however simple it may be, is quite worth knowing. The busy manufacturing town, with its tens and hundreds of thousands of people, where all is movement and bustle, has its history; and the lonely country village, where everybody knows everybody else, has often a history even more interesting than that of the big town—if we only knew what to look for, and where to look for it.

One summer day, years ago, a party of tourists was climbing Helvellyn. One of the party was an elderly gentleman, who was particularly active, and anxious to get to the top. After several hours' stiff climbing the party reached the summit; and there, spread out before them, was a lovely view of hills and dales, of mountains and lakes. Most of the party gazed upon this fair scene in quiet enjoyment; but our old gentleman, as soon as he had recovered his breath, and mopped his red face with his pocket-handkerchief, gave one look round, and then said in a grieved tone: "Is that all? Nothing to see! Wish I hadn't come."

He saw nothing interesting, because he did not know what to look for, and he might just as well have stopped at the bottom. He came to see nothing, *and he saw it.*

CHAPTER II

Men who lived in Caves and Pits

Man is a very ancient creature. It is a curious fact that we have learned most of what we know about the earliest men from the rubbish which they have left behind them. Even nowadays, in this twentieth century, without knowing much about a boy personally, we can tell a good deal about his habits from the treasures he turns out of his pockets. Hard-hearted mothers and teachers call these treasures rubbish, but the contents of a lad's pockets are a pretty sure indication of the boy's tastes, and in what things he is interested.

The earliest traces of the existence of man in our part of the world are found in some places which are now many feet above the level of the sea. There, in the gravel, are the roughly-chipped stone tools and weapons which those early men used, tools which they lost or threw away. Almost every other trace has quite disappeared. Remains belonging to the same period have been noticed in caves in various parts of the world.

The illustration on p. 5 shows two of these very early stone weapons. You will find collections of these, and also of later weapons, in any good museum. These earliest sorts are usually labelled "Palæolithic Stone Implements". The curator of such a museum, we may almost certainly say, would be willing to help you to see the specimens which he has under his care, and you would learn more about them in that way than by just glancing at a picture.

Here, in Britain, caves have been found where these early men have left their stone implements and remains of their rubbish. Some of the best known of such cave-dwellings in Britain are near Denbigh and St. Asaph in North Wales, at Uphill in Somersetshire, at King's Car and Victoria Cave near Settle, at Robin Hood's Cave and Pinhole in Derbyshire, in Pembrokeshire, in King Arthur's Cave in Monmouthshire, at Durdham Down near Bristol, near Oban, and in the gravels in the valleys of the Rivers Trent, Nore, and Dove, in the Irish River Blackwater, near Caithness, and in a good many other places.

So, you see, the remains of these early men cover a pretty wide area. In thinking of the life of those early days we must remember that the aspect of Britain was very different then from what it is now, for in that far-back time these islands were a part of the Continent of Europe, and the North Sea and English Channel were just valleys, with rivers flowing through them, tributaries of the Rhine. There were no insurmountable obstacles to cross between the Continent and these regions, and animals and early man gradually roamed into this part of the world. Geology teaches us a good deal concerning the changes the surface of the ground has undergone. The land was very much higher than it is now—Snowdon, for instance, was at least six hundred feet higher then—and the climate was very much colder. That race of men, apparently, has quite died out. In the course of ages rivers and seas have flowed over the places where these stone tools had been dropped, and, year after year throughout the ages, the drift brought down by the rivers covered them inch by inch and foot by foot. Great changes have taken place in the surface of the land, some suddenly, but most of them very, very slowly. The land has risen, and sunk again, and long, long ages of sunshine and storm, of ice and snow, of stormy wind and tempest, have altered the surface of the country.

Those very ancient men, who lived in the Early Stone Age, are called Cave-dwellers, because they lived apparently in caves, and River-drift Men and Lake-dwellers, because the roughly chipped tools are found in the *drift* of various rivers and lakes.

The Cave-man's weapons and tools were made of chipped flint, which he found broken on the surface of the ground, and these he chipped into shape. They are usually more or less oval, sometimes roughly in the form of a spear-head. Others are borers, or awls, for piercing holes in skins. For rougher work he had hammer-stones, with flat edges, and sharp bits of stone for scrapers. Amongst many other places where these relics have been found in considerable numbers is the Thames valley. They are met with in the higher gravels, on levels now many feet higher than they were in the Cave-man's day, for the surface has risen considerably; and we conclude that there must have been a good many of these people in that neighbourhood.

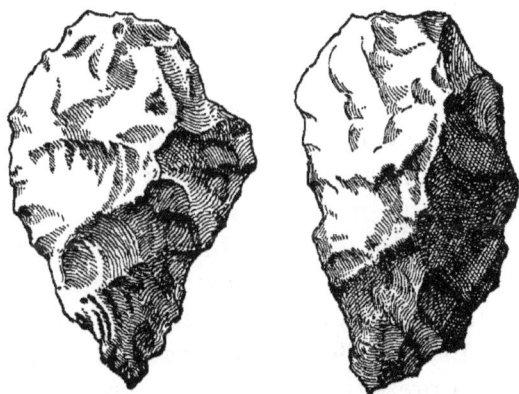

Chipped Flint Weapons

CHAPTER III

The Pit-dwellers

Other remains, not so ancient as these oldest stone implements but still very ancient, are found nearer the surface than the remains of the River-drift Men. They are the remains of people who, like the Drift-men, knew nothing of metals; and they, too, used stone weapons and tools, but these were now better made. They had learned to shape and finish their tools by rubbing, grinding, and polishing them, and they were a much more advanced race of men than the Cave- or Drift-men. These later men, Neolithic Men, did not depend upon the broken and chipped flints which they found lying about on the surface, but discovered that it was better to dig up whole flints, and to select those which were best suited for their purpose, grinding them into the shapes which they wanted, and then polishing them into more shapely and finished weapons.

For the most part we have to go to somewhat desolate parts of England to find traces of them now. In fact those traces would long ago have disappeared had they not been in places which were so wild and difficult to get at that it was not worth any man's while to cultivate them. The spade and the plough would very soon remove all traces of them. In fact, the plough *has* removed many traces of these ancient men, and most of the specimens of their tools and weapons, which you can see in museums, were found by men whilst employed in ploughing and preparing the land for crops.

You must not suppose that we can fix a date when these men first appeared, as we can fix an exact date for the landing of Julius Cæsar, or the sealing of Magna Carta. Neither can we say for how many centuries

they occupied land in what we now call Britain. It was
a long period, at any rate, and during that time their
manners and their customs changed very, very slowly.

The lowest forms of savage life seem very much alike
all the world over. Savages are hunters, and do not as
a rule cultivate the soil. Now hunters must follow their
prey from place to place, so that we should expect these
early men to have no settled homes. But even the
earliest Pit-men had advanced beyond this lowest
stage, for they had flocks and herds, and dogs. They
found out that they could tame some of the animals
which they came across, and that they could use them in
various ways which the earlier men had not thought of.
They need not always go a-hunting for their food, and
they could have a supply at hand if they looked after it.
They discovered that they had a use for the wool and
the milk which these animals yielded, and so they
developed into being a pastoral people, owning flocks
and herds. Then, too, they hit upon the art of making
rough pottery from clay, shaping the various vessels
which they wanted by hand, and baking them in a fire
to harden them. It seems that they found out a way to
spin thread from the wool, and also discovered how to
weave it into a kind of rough cloth, although they used
skins for garments. No doubt these folk hunted as well;
but they were mainly a pastoral people, and at first did
not till the soil. Races of men who did not till the soil
are called Non-Aryan. They chose for their settlements
the tops of hills, and avoided the narrow valleys and low-
lying lands.

The Pit-dwellers are so called from the simple fact
that they had their homes in pits—not, however, dug
anywhere and anyhow. The hole in the ground is the
simplest notion of a house. When in your summer holiday by the sea you see the little boys and girls digging
deep holes in the sand to make "houses", they are

doing in play what the early Pit-dwellers did in real earnest.

The pits were usually some six or eight feet in diameter, and they probably had cone-shaped roofs, formed by poles tied together and covered with peat. In the centre of the hut was the hearth, which was made of flints carefully placed together. The hut would hold two or three people, and the fire on the hearth was its most important feature. The hut in the centre of the group belonged to the head of the family, and other huts were ranged round it.

Surrounding the group was an earthen rampart for further protection, and these earthworks can still be traced in many parts of the country. The huts have gone, of course, and all that can be seen in most cases now is a number of circular patches in the turf, slightly hollowed. People living in the neighbourhood will very likely speak of them as "fairy rings". It is from a careful examination of these hollows that learned men have been able to gather much information concerning the habits of these Pit-dwellers.

We English folk speak proudly of "hearth and home"; they are the centre of our social life, and the idea has come down to us through all these long, long ages. The hearth and the fire upon it was the centre of the life of these men, and the head of a family was also its priest.

Some of the best known of these pit-dwellings are found near Brighthampton, in Oxfordshire; at Worlebury, near Weston-super-Mare; and along the Cotswolds, looking over the Severn valley; and at Hurstbourne, in Hampshire.

At this last place "nine of these early habitations were discovered, some of which were roughly pitched with flint-stones, and had passages leading into the pit. A few flints irregularly placed, together with wood ashes,

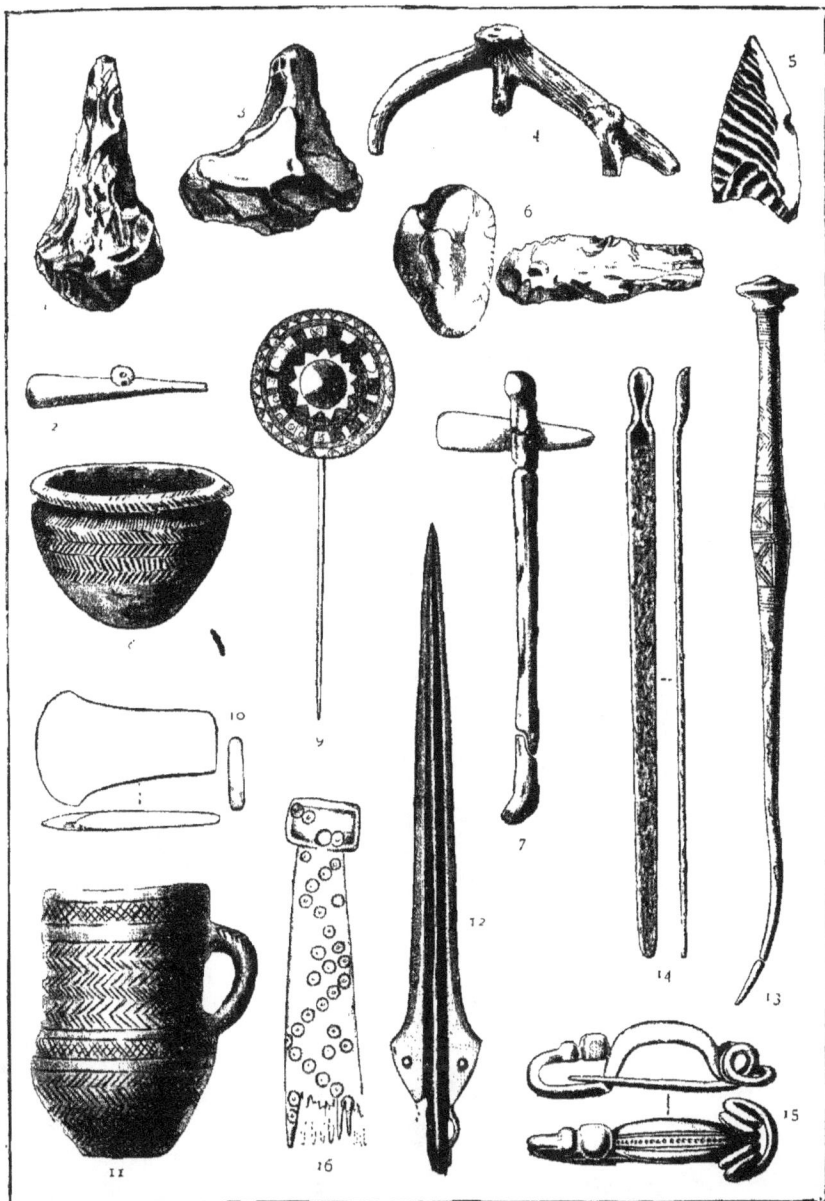

IMPLEMENTS AND ORNAMENTS OF STONE, BRONZE, AND IRON AGES

Older Stone Age: 1. Flint pick (Thames). 2. Bone pendant (Devon). 3. Scraper (Kent). Later Stone Age: 4. Deer antler pick (Norfolk). 5. Arrow-head (Yorkshire). 6. Flint and pyrites for striking fire (Yorkshire). 7. Celt in original haft (Solway Moss). 8. Bowl (Thames). Bronze Age: 9. Pin (Ireland). 10. Celt. 11. Drinking-cup (Berkshire). 12. Spear-head (Thames). 13. Pin (Thames). Early Iron Age: 14. Iron currency-bars. 15. Brooch (Dorset). 16. Hand comb for weaving (Hampshire).

showed the position of the hearths, where cooking operations had been carried on. The sloping entrance passages are peculiar and almost unique in England, though
several have been met with in France."[1]

In the course of time this race seems to have learned
something in the way of cultivating the ground. The
hill-tops, where they built their huts, were only suited
for their cattle, and in order to find soil which they could
till they had to go outside their earthwork, and some
distance down the hill-slope. By their way of digging
the ground, they gradually, in the course of many years,
carved broad terraces, one below the other, on the hill-
sides. There are some very marked traces of such
terraces still to be seen near Hitchin and Luton.[2]

But Pit-dwellings were not the only habitations.
There were Lake-dwellings. One was found in the
year 1892, near Glastonbury, where sixty circular
mounds were noted, each the remains of a Lake-
dwelling, in an area of three acres. There is another
at Hedsor, in Buckinghamshire; and such Lake-
dwellings, of much later periods, have been found in
other parts of the world, and are met with yet in some
parts of South America on the big rivers there; in the
Island of Borneo, in the Caroline Islands, and on the
Gold Coast of Africa.

These dwelling-places of the Lake-dwellers were set
up on sharpened stakes, or piles, driven into the bed of
the lake or river. On these piles a platform was laid,
upon which a wooden hut of wattle and daub was built,
and a rough kind of bridge connected the dwelling with
the shore.[3]

In the course of time—how long ago it is still quite im-

---

[1] *English Villages*, P. H. Ditchfield.
[2] Also between Hitchin and Cambridge, at Clothall, in Herts, on the Chiltern
Hills, on the steep side of the Sussex Downs, in Clun Forest, in Carmarthenshire,
and in Wilts.   [3] See p. 10.

possible to say—a race of men, more advanced than these early Pit-dwellers, found their way to this part of the world. They were more civilized, and were Aryans; that is, they were cultivators of the soil. You may be pretty sure that fighting took place between the two races.

The newer race preferred to make their settlements near running streams. In the middle of each settlement there would be an open space, or meeting-ground, usually a small hill or a mound, round which their huts were built. Beyond this was the garden-ground, then the ground where the grain was grown, and beyond that the grazing-lands. These men began cultivating at the bottom of the hill-sides and valleys, and, as they required more ground, they would advance higher up the slopes.

Gradually to this race came the knowledge of metals, and at that point we reach the Bronze Age. Although polished stone implements were still in use, men had begun to make spear-heads, chisels, and daggers of bronze, which is an alloy of copper and tin. What a great discovery that was, and how we should like to know how the discovery came to be made! It shows a vast advance in intelligence, power of observation, and perseverance in making experiments. This advance gradually led them on to the discovery of the tougher qualities of iron, and how to " get at it ", and to make use of it. Thus we reach the Iron Age.

Lake-dwelling

CHAPTER IV

Earthworks, Mounds, Barrows, &c.

There are still remaining, in many parts of the country, curious mounds and stones. We can say very little about them here; for, though learned men have discovered much, there is still a good deal to be explained concerning them. Old-world stories put most of these strange objects down to the work of witches, fairies, or giants; some ascribe them to the Romans, or to Oliver Cromwell, others even to the devil. But most of them really belong to this period of which we are speaking—the very early part of our history, of which there is no written record.

Earthworks are of many kinds, but the very earliest are usually found on hill-tops. There are some which enclose considerable spaces of ground, bounded by an earthen rampart, with a ditch outside. Sometimes there are two such ramparts. Frequently they are spoken of as British Towns or British Camps. They appear to have been enclosures into which the cattle were driven in time of danger, and in which a whole tribe could take refuge and hold out against their enemies.

Then there are big mounds or heaps, called Barrows. All over the world, not only in Europe, but in northern Asia, in India, and in America, burial-mounds of various sizes have been met with. Some of these are oval in shape, and are called Long Barrows; others are round, and are called Round Barrows. The Long Barrows are thought to be the older kind, and were apparently the burial-places of great leaders. The Round Barrows were also burial-places, but those who raised them burned their dead. The great pyramids of Egypt are barrows, only they are made of stone, not of earth.

At Silbury, in Wilts, there is a huge mound, covering about five acres of ground and some one hundred
and thirty feet in height.

Many interesting things have been brought to light
when these many varieties of barrows have been properly
and scientifically explored by men who have the knowledge and intelligence to "see" what there is to see, and
who do not attack these old earthworks with the idea of

Round Barrow

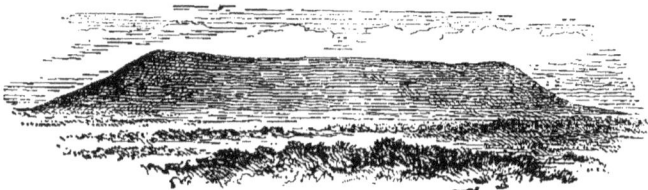

Long Barrow

coming upon some long-hidden hoard of gold or silver.
Indeed, much damage has been done by folk who, from
time to time, have rifled these mysterious old earthworks with that one, sordid idea.   There is much yet
to be done in the way of scientific exploration, and much
to be learned.

The circles of stones at Stonehenge and Avebury seem
to have been connected with the worship of these early
people.

A writer, who has given much attention and study to

STONEHENGE

the subject, gives us some idea as to how these huge stones were got into position at Stonehenge. He thinks that they must have been dragged thither by enormous numbers of men from the Marlborough Downs. "Trunks of trees . . . pierced with holes for levers would furnish rollers to propel the stones to very near their destination. Then it is necessary to suppose the site of Stonehenge occupied by a mound, artificial or natural, the ascent being by an easy incline from the quarter whence these stones were brought. On the top of the mound we must suppose as many holes dug as there were upright stones to be placed. On the arrival of each stone it would be dropped into its hole; and, when all were thus placed, there would only remain the more easy task of laying on the imposts, each end of which has evidently been mortised on to the perpendiculars. The earth would then be dug away, leaving the structure complete."[1]

In 1918 Stonehenge was given to the nation, and we may hope that what is left of it will be carefully preserved in the time to come.

Avebury appears to have been made up of a vast circle of unhewn stones enclosing two other separate double circles. They are in ruins now, and more than six hundred and fifty of these huge stones have been destroyed. There are now standing upright only fifteen; sixteen have been overthrown, and eighteen are known to be buried. It seems that folk, who did not understand or care about these very ancient stones, broke them up and carried the pieces away to make boundary walls or to mend roads, and for any other purpose as they thought fit.

The remains at Avebury are believed to be much older than those at Stonehenge, dating back a thousand years or so before Christ. Those at Stonehenge, which covers

---

[1] W. Long, in the *Wilts Arch. Mag.*, p. 121.

a very much smaller area, seem to belong to the Iron Age, some two hundred years before Christ.

There are many single stones, especially in Cornwall and Wales, which also seem to have been connected with religious rites, but of this we know nothing for certain. Some are Dolmens—flat stones, each on four uprights. In later times they have served as boundary marks.

In various parts of England there are deep lanes or cuttings, which have received curious local names. There are no less than twenty-two such cuttings in different parts of England all known as Grim's Ditch. These, no doubt, formed boundaries, separating various tribes.

The White Horse, cut out of the slope of Uffington Hill, and several similar objects in Wiltshire, as well as the crosses—also cut in the turf—at Whiteleaf and Bledlow, may also belong to this period. Some learned men, however, have thought that they are of a later date.

From these early men, then, the Ancient Britons appear to have descended, and they were settled here a good many centuries before the coming of the Romans. Many of the wild tales and legends still told in country villages, about giants and fairies, have come down to us from these early times.

Dolmen at Plas Newydd, Anglesea. The scene of Druidical religious rites

CHAPTER V

In Roman Times

Here, then, at the time the Romans first came to Britain, were tribes of Britons who had been established in the country for centuries, living their lives according to the customs of their forefathers, and more or less cultivating the land. The Romans invaded the country, and, in time, subdued the people. They remained masters here for nearly four hundred years, but they did not make such a permanent impression on this country as they did on France and Spain.

We are to-day masters of India, but we have not made India English, nor are we trying to do so. The natives there go on cultivating the land according to their custom from time out of mind. They preserve their own manners, customs, and religions. In places where they come much in contact with our fellow-countrymen they are influenced to a certain degree; but in India to-day the English and the natives lead their own lives, each race quite apart from the others.

So it was with the Romans in Britain. They formed colonies in various places and built towns all over the land; they had country villas dotted here and there, some little distance from the chief towns, and built strong military stations in suitable districts. These posts were kept in communication by means of good roads.

To trace out the network of Roman roads is a study in itself, and much has been learned therefrom. Some roads are still quite easy to trace, as far as their course is concerned, for many of our great main roads to-day run upon the top of them; and from time to time, when excavations are being made for sewers, or for laying water-pipes, or tubes for trunk lines of telephones, the actual metal and foundations of the Roman tracks are found, many feet below the present level of the road. It is sometimes stated that the Roman roads were always straight, and that all obstacles were cleared to make room for them. Whilst it is quite true that this "straightness" and directness was one of the characteristics of these roads, the makers of them were skilled engineers, and they not infrequently found that some older trackway, not particularly straight, was better suited for their purpose, as it avoided some of the natural difficulties of the country. When they used these older ways they took care to raise the surface and lay the metal on firm foundations, so that the traffic along them could be as rapid as along the new, straight roads—and the Romans were great people for getting about rapidly from point to point. One of the most frequent deposits of "rubbish" which the Romans have left behind is "oyster shells", often met with in quantities. They are found in places many miles away from the river-mouths where the oysters were cultivated; so that the question arises: "How did these shells get there?" Either they must have been brought very rapidly from the coast far inland, or the eaters of them did not mind eating them when they were very "high". At any rate, there the shells have been found, showing that distance was no obstacle in the way of getting, not only the things which they reckoned to be necessaries, but expensive luxuries as well. Although the main Roman roads are still in use, there are a great number of cross-roads, which for centuries have been out of use, and their exact courses can only be traced with difficulty, passing as they do through what are now quiet, secluded places, long overgrown by grass and underwood and cultivated fields.

Many Britons must in the course of time have adopted

Roman ways and Roman civilization; but the bulk of the Britons, living away from the Roman centres, kept to their own customs, and cultivated the ground in the way their ancestors had done. They prospered, on the whole, as the Romans kept the various tribes from quarrelling with one another.

No doubt, in districts such as that which we now call Hampshire, and along the Thames valley, where wealthy Romans had their country villas, Roman methods of farming were in use. The Britons would see something of Roman ways of doing things, and perhaps tried to copy them.

But the Romans have not left many marks upon our towns and villages. It is quite true that a large number of our present towns and cities are on the *sites* of, or near, Roman towns; but, in most cases, we have to dig down into the earth to find Roman remains. The most important Roman city, Verulam, has quite disappeared, and the most complete remains of a Roman town, Silchester, are near to what is now a quiet country village. The present cities of London, Winchester, Gloucester, Lincoln, Chester, Carlisle, and the towns of Colchester and Leicester, and several others, can hardly be said to have sprung from Roman towns, though they stand on their sites.

Most of the Roman cities were built in districts where the Britons had been strong, or where they were likely to give trouble. Carlisle and Gloucester were, for instance, military towns because they were on the borders of the Roman territory. London and Winchester were trading cities, and they developed much in Roman times.

But, when the Roman power was withdrawn, there was, in those cities at any rate, a British population which had adopted very extensively Roman customs and ideas. For a time things went on much as they had done while the Romans were here; in fact, until the struggles with the Saxons began.

As a matter of fact, the coming of the Saxons began a good while before the Romans actually left. Various tribes of Saxons attacked different parts of the coast, and with varying success. Colchester had to keep a sharp look-out for them on the east coast; and the Romans built Portchester Castle, in Hampshire, to guard the south coast.

Christianity had found its way to Britain during Roman times, and that helped in the work of civilizing the Britons. But we do not know very much of the early British Church. Christianity probably made more headway among the population in and near the Roman towns than in the wilder districts. The foundations of an early Christian church have been found at Silchester.

Silchester was a very important Roman town, although now, as we have noted, but a small village stands on the spot. Much careful excavation work has been carried on there, and more is known of this Roman city than of any other in England. Other sites of Roman cities are waiting a similar careful exploration, amongst them Verulam, by the city of St. Alban.

Roman Pottery Kiln found at Castor, Hunts

CHAPTER VI

Early Saxon Times

The conquest of South Britain by the Saxons took a long time—considerably over one hundred and fifty years. A great many people are born, and live their lives, and die, in such a period of time as that. It was only little by little that the various tribes of Saxons got a footing in England. They were the stronger and fiercer race, and the Britons were gradually subdued or driven into the mountainous regions by them.

Those early tribes of Saxons, who came to Britain, brought with them, of course, their own special manners and customs. As they settled down, the face of the country was gradually changed by them. They disliked and suspected everything Roman, and destroyed the towns and villas. They hated the idea of walled towns. These, therefore, were left in ruins, and the great highways, being neglected in most places, were, in the course of years, overgrown with brushwood and hidden in thick forests.

In some parts of the country the Saxons seem to have completely swept the Britons away, and almost all traces of them vanished; but in other parts there certainly were some of them left, because we have still their marks upon our language. Although most of the place-names in use now are Saxon or Danish, there are still a good many of British, or partly British, origin.

The names of many of our rivers are British or Celtic, such as Axe, Exe, Stour, Ouse, and Yare. So are many names of hills; and in some parts of the country the names of the villages are partly British and partly Saxon. Take, for instance, such a common name as Ashwell. Some learned men think that it is made up

of two words "Ash" and "Well", both meaning pretty
much the same thing, *ash* being British for "water",
and *well* being Saxon for "watering-place". Now, if
the Saxons had quite got rid of the Britons, they would
not have known that a particular place was called
"Ash"—they learned to call it "Ash" from the natives,
but they did not know what it meant. They knew that
there was a spring of water there, which they called a
"well"; and so, to distinguish it from other wells in
the neighbourhood, they got into the habit of calling
it "Ashwell"—and the name has stuck to the place.
In North America, in Australia, New Zealand, and
South Africa there are many instances of English
names being grafted on to original native names, and
often you find places with well-known English names
and others with picturesque and descriptive native names
almost side by side.

In some such way as this many other place-names,
partly British and partly Saxon, were formed; and they
teach us this—that Saxons and Britons must have lived
near each other closely enough for the Saxons to take
up and use some British names.

There are some English counties in which you will
hardly find one place-name which is not Saxon. This
shows us that the Britons were either killed or completely driven away. That is the case in Hertfordshire.
But in Hampshire, while most of the names are Saxon,
there are many partly Saxon and partly British. The
same thing can be noticed in the county of Gloucester.
The Britons, then, must have been in these districts
long enough for the Saxons to pick up a good many
place-names. They did not understand the meaning of
them, and so tacked on to them names which they *did*
understand, much as British settlers have done in various
parts of the world during these last few centuries.

The place-names of the old towns and villages all

REMAINS OF A ROMAN HOUSE, EXCAVATED AT SILCHESTER

[See page 17]

had a meaning, and when we can get to know what that meaning is it tells us something of the history of the place. But we have to be very careful in studying place-names not to jump to conclusions as to what the name means. To get at the truth a knowledge of the old language and the alterations it has undergone, and also of the different ways in which the word was spelt, according to the earliest documents that can be found, is necessary. In days gone by, before the study of the old forms of the language was properly grasped, antiquaries often made guesses at the meaning of place-names which have turned out to be very misleading. So we must not be in a hurry to jump to conclusions, and should be always on the look-out for more and better information. We frequently meet with the syllable *ing* in a place-name. "Ing", amongst those early Saxon settlers here, usually meant "the sons of". When they made a new home in this strange land the little band naturally gave the place the name of their family. Thus, the sons of a man named Offa were known as Uffingas, and called the name of the place where they settled Uffinggaston, or Uffington—and the name stuck to the place long after the family itself had died out. The sons of Rede settled at Reading; the sons of Billinge, the Billings, at Billingham; the sons of Hôc at Woking and Wokingham; the Ardings at Ardington; the Thurings at Thorington—and so on. You must not, however, conclude that every name you come across with "ing" in it has the same meaning; but it will be quite worth while to ask for information about it from someone who knows, or who can put you in the way of getting information upon the point.

We cannot go further here into other syllables found in a large number of place-names, such as *feld*, *yard*, *stock* or *stoke*, or *ham*, but it is quite possible for you to find out first of all what is the meaning of the name of the town or village in which you live, and what that tells you about its history.

The Saxons made their settlements at first away from the Roman towns and British villages. In the course of time, in a good many cases, they made settlements very close to these old sites, and we know that Saxons lived in such places as Winchester, Gloucester, and London. We find, especially in Hampshire and Gloucestershire, that near, or in, certain villages with Saxon names, Roman remains have from time to time been dug up.

CHAPTER VII

Early Saxon Villages

It is with the coming of the Saxons that the history of our towns and villages really begins. For, though there are not a few places which show some connection with Romans, Britons, and Pit-dwellers, it is mainly from Saxon times that we can follow the history of the places in which we live, with any certainty.

When the Saxons came to Britain they brought their own ideas with them, of course. Nowadays, when English folk go to settle in a distant land, they take their English notions with them. They find, however, in the course of time, that they have to modify or alter them somewhat, according to the circumstances in which they are placed. They may find that roast beef and plum-pudding do not at all suit them in the new climate. If they are wise, they will see whether the food-stuffs used by the natives, and folk who have lived out there for many years, are not more suitable, even though they may be inclined to despise such food at first.

Now the Saxon tribes which first settled in England

in the fifth century belonged to a race of people bold, strong, fierce, and free. But they could not make their new homes exactly what their old ones had been in the land whence they had come.

Like those other Aryan people, who had made their way to Britain in the Stone Age, they lived together in families. When the family became too large, some of the members had to turn out, like bees from a hive, though not in such great numbers, and set out on their travels to form new settlements, or village communities.

This idea of a village community had come down to them through many generations. The early Saxon idea of a village community was something of this sort:—

All the men of the family had equal rights; though there was one who was head of the family, and who took the lead. The affairs of the family were discussed and settled at open-air meetings, called folk-moots. The spot where these were held was regarded as a sacred place. The tilling of their land, their marriages, their quarrels, their joining with other villages to make war or peace, were all settled at the folk-moot. The question whether the younger branches of the family should leave the village and go out and form another was fixed by the folk-moot also. In the course of time many such little swarms left the parent hive, and settled farther away.

But they always looked back upon the old settlement as their home, and the head of the family as their chief. They were all of one *kin*, and in the course of time they began to look upon their chief as their king.

Now what was the nature of the old Saxon village settlement? In its general arrangement it was very like the old Pit-dwellers' settle-

Saxon Brooch found at Abingdon, made of gold encrusted with coloured glass

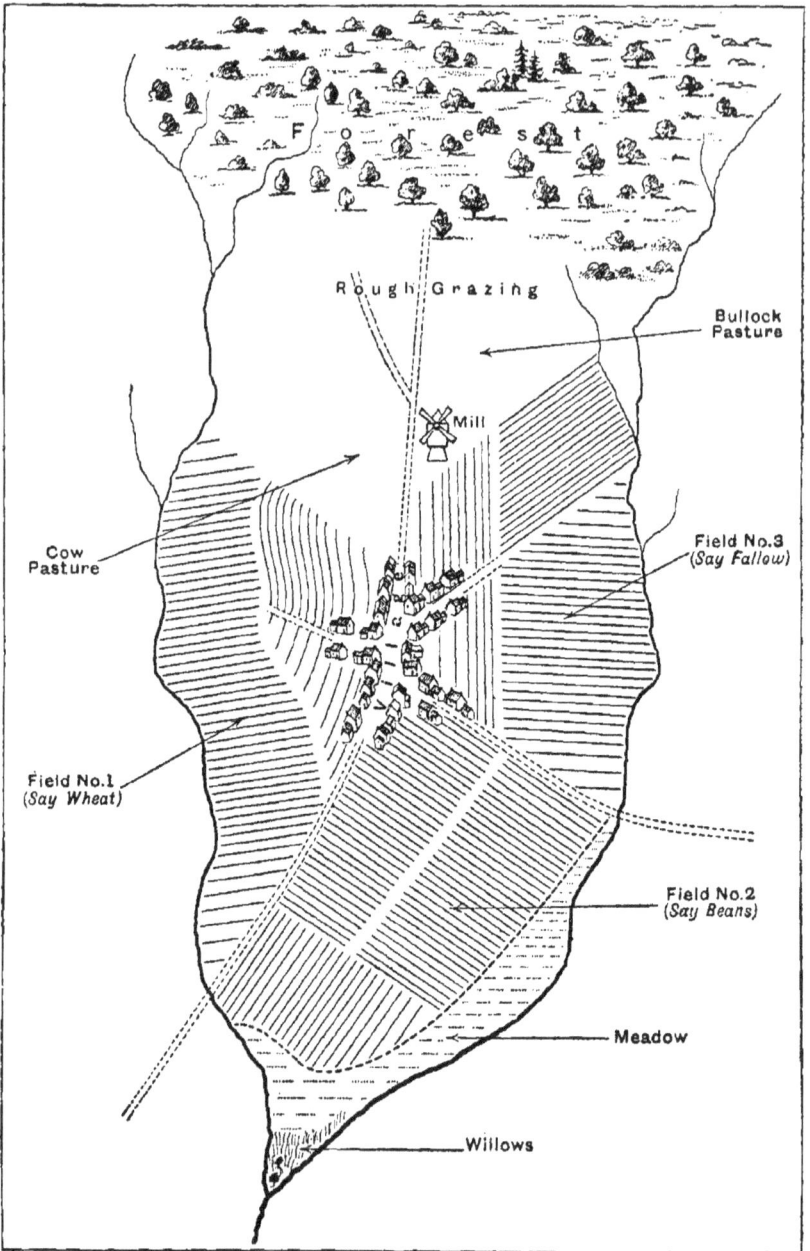

Diagram of a Saxon Village Settlement

ment. There was the open space where the men of the village met, the sacred mound where the folk-moot was held. The houses in which the family dwelt were placed close together, round the hut of the head of the family.

Outside these was a paling of some sort, so that all the houses were within the enclosure, or "tun", as it was called; and here calves and other young stock were reared near the houses. Beyond the enclosure, or tun, was the open pasture-ground and the arable land, or land under cultivation. Beyond these would be the untouched forest-land, or open moorland.

Each man of the tun had a share in these lands; not to do with as he liked, but to use according to the custom of his family. The arable land was divided into strips, and shared amongst the men. However many strips of land a man might have, he could not have them for all time. The strips were apparently chosen by lot, and changed from time to time, so that all had an equal chance in having the best land. In the same way the number of cattle a man might turn out to graze on the pasture-land was regulated. The folk-moot, or meeting of the people, was a very important assembly, and through it the little community was governed.

Such was the mode of life to which the Saxons who came to England had been used; but they were not nearly as free when they landed here as their ancestors had been. More and more power had come into the hands of the chief or king, and to him the people looked for protection and guidance. In times of war, or when the tribe was invading new lands, the power of the king increased. By the time, then, that the Saxon tribes began their settlement in England, they were very much under the rule of their chiefs or kings. The kings had rights and powers over their followers which had gradually grown up by long custom, and none of those followers ventured to dispute such rights and powers.

CHAPTER VIII

Anglo-Saxon Tuns and Vills

A good many Britons no doubt settled down with the Saxons as slaves, and that probably accounts for so many of the natural features of the country—the rivers and the hills—keeping their old British names. The British villages must have had names, but those villages were apparently destroyed, and the slaves would be settled near the homesteads which the conquerors set up.

In fixing on a place for a "tun" the Saxons would choose a valley rather than a hill, usually near a running stream, or a plentiful supply of water. At the present time nearly all over England we can find villages which have not been touched by modern improvements and alterations, and most of these show something even now of their Saxon origin.

For instance, in the county of Rutland there is a village named Exton, which has for many centuries kept several features which show its connection with Saxon days. Its name, Ex-ton, seems to be compounded of the British word "ex", which means "water", and the Saxon "ton" or "tun", which means the "enclosure."—"the tun by the water". There, sure enough, flowing by the village, is a stream, a tributary of the River Gwash; just such a stream as the Saxons loved. In the middle of the village is the triangular open space, or village green. Round it the houses are thickly clustered together, with hardly any garden ground at the back or in front, and most of them with none at all. Outside the ring of houses are small grass fields or closes, where calves and cows feed, and poultry run. These little fields form a kind of ring round the village, and the hedges enclosing them represent the old fence of Saxon days, which formed the "tun". Beyond this are wider pasture-grounds and big plough-lands, stretching away in several directions up the gentle slopes.

You will be able to find a good many villages which have some resemblance to Exton; they answer very closely to the Anglo-Saxon vill and the Anglo-Saxon town, for town and village were laid out on the same principle.

Now look at some little sleepy country town, and you will see much the same arrangement as in the village. The wide open space in the middle, where the town pump stands, and where the market is held, answers to the village green. Though this is often spoken of as the Market Square, it is usually more like a triangle in shape than a square.

The old houses round the market square are built very closely one into the other, and with queer narrow alleys leading to houses behind those in front; much in the same way as the houses are clustered round the village green. Round the outskirts of the town, at the back of the houses, are small green closes or paddocks. Beyond them are the larger meadows and pastures; then the wide corn-lands and woods; and, not far away, the heath or common.

The Saxon settlements, the "tuns" or "vills", whether they afterwards became what we now understand as "towns" or "cities", or remained what we call villages, had all the same chief features. Just as ordinary schoolrooms and railway stations are all pretty much alike, because they all have to serve much the same purpose, so the Saxon settlements were very similar in their general plan.

There was the open place, where people met and the folk-moot was held, surrounded by the houses of stone or wood in which the people lived. Around these lay the grass yards or common homestead; and, beyond them, the wide arable and pasture-lands, with patches of moorland and forest.

But outside the actual "tun" there would be something connected with the Saxon settlement which you would be sure to notice. After you had passed the boundary to the tun, you would see no hedgerows or walls dividing the land into fields. The arable land was one huge field. Its position would depend, of course, upon the nature of the soil and the lie of the land. You would not expect to find it down in the water-meadows, through which the river flowed ; it would be higher up, out of the reach of floods; perhaps on the hill-sides.

Then you would see the huge field, ploughed in long strips, about a furlong in length, that is, a " furrow long ",[1] and one or two perches in breadth. Between the ploughed strips would be narrow unploughed strips, on which, in places, brambles would grow. The heath-lands and moorlands were uncultivated tracts, where rough timber and underwood grew, which was cut and lopped by the people of the vill under certain conditions. · There were no formal spinneys,[2] nor wide stretches of old timber, such as we nowadays expect to see in a forest. In places the forests contained old timber, and were thick with undergrowth, and infested with wild animals, such as wolves and boars. The name forest was often given to an uncultivated district, not much differing from a rough common, where sheep, cattle, and swine could pick up a living.

---

[1] A furrow, or furlong, was, roughly speaking, the distance the plough would travel up or down the field before it was turned. ·

[2] Spinneys are plantations of trees growing closely together.

THE VILLAGE GREEN, EXTON, RUTLAND

[See page 56]

CHAPTER IX

Tythings and Hundreds—Shires

Though the Saxons, as they settled down in England, formed "tuns", which at first had very little to do with one another, that state of things probably did not last a very long time. In fighting the Britons they had to act together; and, for the sake of protection and help, these separate communities had to combine. Somewhat in this way ten families in a district would form a tything; and the heads of the villages would, from time to time, meet together to consult on various matters in which they were interested.

Then larger areas would need to be covered, as the country became more settled. Ten tythings would make a hundred; and, from time to time, men from all the places in the hundred would meet together and hold hundred courts. The meeting-place for the hundred was always some well-known spot, selected originally because of its convenient situation—some particular tree was a favourite place; and, as the folk met there regularly so many times in the year, the spot was easily kept in mind from one generation to another. At the meeting criminals were tried, disputes settled, and in the later times, when monasteries had become common, some sort of record was often made of the important matters decided upon, and kept with the documents belonging to the monastery, as being a safe place in which to keep them. Scraps of these ancient records have been met with on old parchments which in later times have been used over again for another purpose.

Most of the English counties are still divided into hundreds. In those days the hundreds were not all of the same size, because, owing to the nature of the soil,

some tuns were far apart from one another, and a
tything might cover a wide district, and a hundred a
much larger area. If the hundred was small, that would
show that the tuns were pretty close together, and that
the district was populous. If, on the other hand, the
tythings and hundreds were large, that would show that
the district was thinly peopled.

We have seen that new settlements were formed by
portions of the family leaving the old home, and making
a new tun in the most suitable place they could find.
It would happen, no doubt, in favourable districts, that
new tuns would spring up not very far from the mother
tun; and, in the course of time, there would be a good
many more tuns in the tything than there were originally.
The fact seems to be, that when once the boundaries
had been roughly agreed upon, they were not often
altered. From being a combination of families, or tuns,
the tything got to be a district; and it kept its name
of tything long after the number of tuns in it had
increased.

It was much the same with the hundreds. In time
they were represented by certain districts, whose borders
were known to the people living in them. The hundreds
all over the country have not altered their boundaries to
any great extent until quite recently. In Hampshire
to-day there are thirty-seven hundreds; in Hertfordshire
there are only eight; and Middlesex has now the same
six hundreds which it had twelve centuries ago when a
good part of the county was forest land.

As to the time when the hundreds became grouped
into shires we cannot speak definitely; the change was
brought about gradually and quite naturally. It is not
at all likely that all the various kingdoms in England
came together on some particular occasion and said:
"Now we'll divide all our kingdoms into shires". But
the hundreds did become grouped into shires, doubtless

Ploughing. From an old Saxon Calendar in the British Museum

because it was necessary that they might act together in matters which concerned all.

There is nothing like a threatened danger from without to draw men together. We have seen this in a most remarkable way during the Great War. In the tun, no doubt, the villagers fell out with each other; however fairly the strips of land were shared somebody was sure to get what he did not like, and to grumble about it. Some of his fellow-villagers would take his side, and say it was a shame; and others would take the opposite side. But if the cattle belonging to the tun over the hills, or on the other side of the marsh, had been seen on the wrong side of the mark, or boundary which separated the lands of the two tuns, the dispute about the strips in the field would be forgotten, and away the people would go in a body towards the offending tun "to see about it".

In much the same way, when the boundaries of a tything or hundred were invaded by another tything or hundred, the differences between the tuns would be dropped, in order to preserve the rights which they had in common.

There was strife among the Saxon kingdoms which lasted for many years, especially between the three great rivals, Wessex, Mercia, and Northumbria. The lesser kingdoms were under the dominion, sometimes of one, sometimes of another of these rivals. All this fighting and settling down put more and more power into the hands of the kings. Instead of each village fighting for itself, and leaving all the others to fight for themselves, it was found to be a much safer and wiser policy to join together for common protection. Now if people join together, whether in peace or war, to win a football match or to take a city, somebody must be in authority to give the necessary orders. Hence the power of the king, and the officers acting under him, grew up *by custom*, until the overlordship of the king was so firmly established that no one dared call it in question.

Apparently from the smaller Saxon kingdoms we get our older shires. Whether the overlord happened to be the King of Mercia, or the King of Wessex, the under-king continued to rule over his old kingdom, or share. When, at length, in the ninth century, the King of Wessex was acknowledged as the overlord or King of England, Wessex and Mercia, and a part of Northumbria, were gradually divided into *shares*, or shires, over each of which the King of England appointed a reeve to look after his interests—the shire-reeve or sheriff. The King of England still appoints the high sheriff of each county. An eorlderman, who, in the case of the older shires, was at first no doubt a descendant of the old under-king, looked after the business of the shire itself.

Amongst the older shires we have Kent, Surrey, Sussex, Essex, Middlesex; while the newer ones were all named after some important central town, which in each case gave its name to the shire; such are Hertfordshire and Bedfordshire. You can easily pick these out from a list of the counties of England at the present time.

CHAPTER X

The Early English Town

At first, as we have seen, the Saxons were an agricultural people, and each village or tun produced all that it needed for its own support. But in peaceful times a tun might produce more than it needed; and by and by something like trade and exchange between one place and another would begin. There were many places, as for example London, which in Roman times had been great places for commerce, to which ships had come bringing various kinds of goods. In time, as the Saxons settled down, they began to have new wants, and some of them began to be attracted towards places where there were more people than in their native tuns. Some men found that they could make certain articles of common use better than their neighbours could. Thus certain trades took their rise. Those who worked at them would gradually give up the agricultural labour in which everybody else in the tun was employed. We do not know the causes which led certain of these agricultural tuns to become trading-places, but it is quite certain that they did gradually grow to be what we now call towns.

We find Saxon towns springing up near the places where some of the Roman towns had been, in some cases on the actual site of the Roman city. In Gloucester and Lincoln, for instance, some of the streets to-day follow the actual lines of the Roman streets. These towns are, however, really Saxon towns, not old Roman towns turned into Saxon towns. The men of these Saxon towns had lands on the outskirts of the towns, just as the village men had. Even to-day you will notice that there are many towns which possess lands called by such names as the Townlands, Townfield, or Lammas Land.

The men in these towns were, from the very first, more inclined to hold out against an overlord than the men in the villages were. In the first place, their numbers were greater; and then they had more varieties of occupation than the villagers, or, as we may say, had wider interests. In the trading towns, like London and Southampton, they came in contact with traders from other lands, and trade brought them more wealth. They, too, had their folk-moots, and they had more business to transact in them than the country villagers had. They were very particular to keep a tight hold on their rights, and were always on the look-out to gain fresh privileges if they possibly could.

The fence or wall, which surrounded the town, was made much stronger than that round the village; and men saw the use now of the thick walls of the old Roman cities which their ancestors had despised, for they had wealth and goods which needed protection.

We have seen that the power of the king gradually increased; and, as it did so, the king and the town became more necessary to each other. The town was wealthy; but it could not stand by itself against all the rest of the country. The king had the power of the country at his back, and could protect it if he would. The town had to give something to the king in return for this protection. But we shall presently see more of the relations between king and town.

CHAPTER XI

In Early Christian Times

One great and important factor in the making of Saxon England was Christianity. The first Saxons who came were heathen, and they wiped out the British Christianity, where they settled, as completely as they wiped out Roman civilization. Towards the end of the sixth century Christian missionaries were at work in the north and in the south of what we now call England, and from that time onwards the Church played an important part in the making of the nation.

So, side by side with the development and political growth of the country came the spread of Christianity and the organization of the Church. We find that the folk in the Saxon kingdoms, following the lead of their kings, became Christian as a matter of course. Over and over again we find the kings giving up Christianity and going back to paganism, and their people following them, also as a matter of course. The conversion of England took many years to accomplish, and mixed up with the Christianity was much paganism, which was not overcome for many centuries. The dioceses[1] of the early Saxon bishops were, roughly speaking, of the same extent as the early kingdoms, and the bishops and their clergy travelled about as missionaries.

As the lords or thanes of the various vills, following the example of their kings, accepted Christianity, their people followed their example. In the open places of the tuns and vills, where the folk-moots were held, Christianity was preached and the cross set up. That, probably, was the origin of most of the village and market crosses.

[1] A diocese is the district over which a bishop rules.

Then, in the course of time, in some cases, a church was built on a part of the old sacred open spaces. You cannot help noticing to-day how in many towns the chief church is by the market-place, and in the villages by the village green. In other cases we find the church and manor-house are outside the present village. That may be because the thane's or lord's land was outside the vill or tun, and he built the church on his own land, not on the common public land in the middle of the tun. It may have happened, also, that at the time the church was first built the houses were there also; but, owing to changes many years afterwards, the people have removed to another spot some distance away—possibly to the side of a busy main road. Then the original village has dwindled away; the houses, having fallen into ruin, have been pulled down, and no trace of them is now left.

A priest would be appointed by the bishop, to work in a tun, and a portion of land would be set apart in the common fields to maintain him and to aid in carrying on the services of the church. In course of time there were certain dues and fees given to him, the paying of which became a recognized custom. Somewhat in this way glebe lands and tithes took their rise, and became a part of the land system of the Saxon people.

Along with the growth of churches in the tuns and vills was the founding of monasteries. Small bodies of men bound themselves by simple rules to live and work and worship together. Frequently they made their settlements in lonely, desolate places, which they worked to bring under cultivation. So there sprang up settlements, or convents, of these religious people, living under their own rules. Work and worship went side by side. It was a new kind of life, different from the life in the "tun" which the early Saxons were used to; but in time it had a mighty influence in the land, and played an important part in the making of England.

CROSS AND CHURCH, GEDDINGTON, NORTHAMPTONSHIRE

[See page 56]

CHAPTER XII

Monasteries

The Saxons learned to respect the quiet simple lives of the early monks. They saw them toiling hard in their fields, bravely facing many difficulties and hardships, and turning the wilderness into a garden. At first each monk, from the abbot downwards, had to take his share in the toil, wherever it was, and the monastery, as well as the vill, had to produce all that it needed.

Men who were not very good or very religious began to respect the lives and works of the monks. We find thanes and kings not only allowing monks to settle on some of their unoccupied land, but making over to them some of their own land, on condition that they and their children after them might always have a share in the prayers of these good men. We see, too, that whole vills came gradually into the hands of some monasteries; so that the convent became the lord of the vill instead of a thane or a king.

Some convents made rapid progress, while others never prospered, but in the course of time disappeared. We have seen that the vill and the " town " grew up in much the same way, and were formed on the same plan. There are, however, a good many towns which grew up round monasteries in the first instance.

For example, King Offa II, at the end of the eighth century, founded the monastery of St. Alban, giving to it a wide extent of land round the ruins of the old city of Verulam. The monastery was built, and much land brought under cultivation. We find the sixth abbot, Ulsinus, two centuries later, encouraging people to settle round the walls of the monastery. That monastery lay near one of the great roads of England; many people were coming and going; so houses were built and a market was established. Churches, too, were erected for the use of the people who settled in the town. The abbot was the lord of this " town ", and the people dwelling in it were his tenants. He, like any other lord of a " tun ", or " vill ", was responsible for the keeping of order and good government on his land.

St. Edmund's Bury, or Bury St. Edmund's, grew up round a monastery which had been established in a lonely place; and there, also, arose in time a flourishing town, under the rule of the abbot.

A number of towns, which to-day are cathedral cities, grew up round the churches where the bishop and his principal clergy had their homes and chief centres of work.

These things only came about very gradually. The monks who settled first at Bury, or those whom King Offa settled by the ruins of Verulam, never dreamed that in the years to come their convents would be great landowners, with many hundreds of tenants. But it was so; and the monasteries at length formed one of the most important classes of landowners in the country; their special rights and privileges coming to them so gradually, and so naturally, that no one realized exactly what was taking place.

Those who entered a monastery, or embraced " the religious life ", intended to keep out of the world, and apart from its cares and worries as much as they could. But the lands left to them had to be looked after and cultivated. These did not always lie close round the monastery—very frequently they were tracts of land in distant counties—and somebody had to look after them. New possessions bring new responsibilities; and so we we find that the monasteries had not only to attend to the daily round of worship and work inside the walls of the monastery, but had to carry on all the business belonging to great estates as well.

So in time a monastery had to use the services of many men besides monks; the monks became great employers of labour one way and another, and this attracted to their towns a good many skilled workmen.

The times when the Danes ravaged the greater part of the country were very trying to the life of English villages and towns. These sea-rovers came, at first, as plunderers, and the destruction of towns, churches, and monasteries was very great. Some monasteries, like Crowland[1], suffered several times, and many were never rebuilt. But gradually the invaders themselves settled in England. They did not bring with them an entirely new land system. As they settled down to farming and village life, we find that land was held in almost exactly the same manner as under Saxon customs.

Of course there were some differences, and those who have studied the subject closely can indicate a good many points in which the Saxon and Danish land customs differed from each other. The dangers to which the Saxons had been exposed by the attacks of the Danes had put a great deal of power into the hands of the thanes and the king. Thus, by the time the Danes had settled in England, every vill and tun had got into the hands of some lord or thane, or was in the king's hands. In Danish settlements there seems always to have been an overlord, who led his people in war and ruled in time of peace; though there was a class of freemen amongst them which had special rights and privileges. You will remember that when King Alfred came to terms with the Danes at the Peace of Wedmore, in the year 880, it was agreed that the part of England east of the old Roman road, Watling

[1] In the Fens.

Street, which ran from London to Chester, should be regarded as Danish territory. In that district you will find a good many Danish place-names as well as the older Saxon place-names—names which end in "by", "ey", "ness", "wic", and "thorpe". A great many will be found in Lincolnshire, Northamptonshire, and farther north. But some will also be found in other parts of the country. For instance; there is in Hampshire, in the valley of the River Meon, quite a little nest of Danish place-names—a fact which shows that Danes settled in that district even in the midst of what may be called a Saxon stronghold.

But the Danes were something more than tillers of the soil; they were traders too, and "tuns" became in many places more like our "towns" and trading-places than ever they had been before. In time we find the largest towns in the Danish part of England—Leicester, Lincoln, Derby, Nottingham, and Stamford—binding themselves together to protect their trading interests.

Saxon Church at Bradford-on-Avon

This little building, one of the earliest stone churches, lay hidden for centuries, but was rediscovered in 1857. The monastery once attached to it has long since perished.

CHAPTER XIII

Towns and Villages in the Time of Cnut the Dane

Now let us see what an ordinary village was like in the time of King Cnut, when Saxon and Dane were living pretty comfortably together, side by side, under good government.

We find that each vill or tun had a lord, an eorl, or thane, who practically owned the place and everything in it, though he could not do entirely as he liked. There was the land which belonged to him, and which was in his own hands, or occupation, as we say; that was called his demesne. The rest of the land was also his, but it was let out to people who had lived on the land from time out of mind—the cheorls or villeins. The lord's house was on his demesne. The villeins' houses were all together in the tun, with the grass yards for the cattle close to them, and the open fields and pasture-lands outside the tun, just as they had been in the olden days.

There seems to have been two classes of villeins— geburs and cottiers.

The geburs were the higher class. They appear very frequently to have held about one hundred and twenty acres of land; they had to work on the lord's home farm two or three days a week, or pay him certain produce of the land as a rent; and they had to provide one or more oxen for the village plough, when there was ploughing to be done on the lord's farm, or in the common field.

In the Danish part of the country there appears to have been a class of freeholders, in some places, called socmen, but there were not very many of them. They, no doubt, had had their rights granted to them for distinguished service in the Danish wars.

The cottiers held only about five acres of land. They had to work for the thane or lord on certain days of the week; but, as they had no oxen, they had no ploughing to do for him.

Below the geburs and the cottiers were the theows, thralls, or slaves, who could be bought and sold. They were captives taken in war, or men who, for their crimes, had been doomed to slavery.

We must remember that the overlord might be the king or a bishop, a monastery or a thane. Their rights over their vills and tuns were much the same in each case, and their duties to those vills and tuns were also similar.

A very large number of vills and tuns were under the lordship of the various bishops and monasteries. It was so with towns like Winchester, Reading, Bury St. Edmund's, and St. Alban's. The custom had grown up quite naturally and in the course of many years.

It is pretty clear that the overlord did not always reside in his vill or tun. The tuns or vills of the bishopric of Winchester, for instance, were scattered about in the various parts of the diocese. It was the same with other overlords. But we find in every place a steward, and in each town the king's reeve or the lord's reeve. These acted for the overlord, whoever he was, and saw that the villeins and cottiers did their proper proportion of work at the right time; they saw that the lord's tolls at the markets, fairs, and ferries, were properly enforced. The steward was a most important officer in every town and village, and a great deal of power was in his hands.

Then in the ordinary country vill there was the faber, or smith; the mason; the pundar, or man who looked

Agriculture. From an eleventh-century manuscript in the British Museum

Below are shown the workers carrying their burdens home at the end of the day.

after the fences and hedges and drove stray cattle into the pound. Then there was the carpenter, and even the bee-keeper, for honey was an important ingredient used in the making of the drink of the community. The simple ordinary trades were found in the country villages then, as they are now; but the craftsmen, the most skilled workmen, had become for the most part dwellers in the towns. Even in very early times we find craftsmen in towns formed into trades' unions or guilds, to protect their special trades.

Now the land was shared amongst the villeins and cottiers in strips, usually containing an acre or half-acre, in the common fields of which we have heard before. The villein did not have all the strips belonging to his holding set out side by side—they lay in different parts of the great open field. Crops had to be sown according to the custom of the vill or tun, and according to a fixed order. Wheat and rye would be sown one year on a part of the great field; barley, oats, and beans the next year; and the third year the land must be left fallow. The lord's land had to be treated in the same way.

On the pasture-land and in the meadows the villein and cottier had the right to turn out a certain number of cattle, according to the size of their holdings. The crops, whether of hay or corn, had to be cleared from the fields by certain fixed days, so that cattle might be turned out to graze. You will still find, in some towns, that certain of the freeholders, or burgesses, have the right to turn a certain number of cattle on certain lands for a part of the year between fixed dates.

Then, on the rough commons or heaths there were also grazing rights for the lord and his tenants. The tenants might "top and lop" the trees growing there at certain times, but they might not cut the trees down—that was the lord's right. There were also rights of cutting turf and heather, and the turning of hogs into the forest; all these rights were ruled by "custom", which bound both the lord and the tenants.

These "customs", although they were very similar, were not the same in every place—each community had its own special "customs" which were clung to most rigidly from generation to generation. However much inclined the lord or his reeve might be to try to get rid of the old "customs" in order to get more power into his own hands, or to make more out of the tenants, he was forced to respect the "custom" of the place or there would be grievous trouble. And it was a good thing that both lords and tenants had thus to respect each the right of the other, for it has helped to foster from the very early days that spirit which makes for liberty, which we value so highly, so that a man may live his life in security and freedom.

The lord, or steward, or reeve, held courts or meetings at regular intervals. At first these took place in the open air, like the old folk-moots; but in time they came to be held in a court-house. The court was a meeting, presided over by the lord or his steward, to see that the customs of the place were kept up; to call to account those tenants who had failed to do their share of the work; to put new tenants into the places of those who had removed or died; and to punish offenders.

This last right, of punishing offenders, was one thought to be of vast importance. In the early days the men of the tun were bound together to keep the peace, and to see that it was kept; and they were strong enough to keep evil-doers in check. In the trading tuns or towns especially the right was valued very highly; but, at the time we are now treating of, the right to exercise punishment was in the hands of the overlord, though the men of the place had still some voice in the government of their town. The right to have a gallows was one eagerly sought for, and held very firmly; not because people particularly wanted to hang one another, but because the gallows represented to them the highest power of government. The towns had lost most of their rights in this respect, but they had never forgotten those they had had, and were always on the alert to get back any lost right, or to gain a new one which should help them to obtain the privilege of self-government.

Ploughing. *From an eleventh-century manuscript in the British Museum*

CHAPTER XIV

Churches and Monasteries in Danish and Later Saxon Times

In speaking of our towns and villages we are obliged to make mention frequently of churches and monasteries. At the time when Cnut was king, each vill or tun had its church and its priest to minister in it. There were parts of the land, in the common fields and pasture, mixed up with the villeins' strips, set apart for the support of the services of the Church, the maintenance of the priest, and the care of the poor. In time various dues and customs were also paid to the priest for certain things which he was expected to do.

There are very few churches still standing which have any parts of their structure dating from before the time of King Cnut. In the early days churches were very simple buildings, built mainly of wood, and in the Danish wars most of them were destroyed.

In the tenth century there was a very general belief that the world was coming to an end at the end of the thousand years after the establishment of Christianity; so there was not much actual church-building going on. But in King Cnut's time a revival of interest in church-building took place, and there are in a good many of the old churches of England little bits of work in the walls, or very rude carvings over the doorways, which belong to this time. Unless such work is pointed out to you by one who understands something about these matters, you will not be likely to discover it for yourself, any more than you are likely to discover the traces of the pit-dwellings, of which we spoke in an early chapter.

These parish churches and parish priests were under

the control of the bishop, who had his chief church or cathedral in some important place in his diocese. Those cathedrals were generally served by colleges of clergy, called canons.

These were the public churches. But besides them there were colleges and monasteries, which were private societies of men living together. Some of the religious

Wooden Church at Greenstead, Essex.   Built in 1013 as a temporary shelter for the body of St. Edmund during its removal from London to Bury.   The illustration is copied from an engraving dated 1748, when the building was entire, though much decayed

houses were in towns, as we have seen, and others were in wild desolate places. Every religious house, whether a monastery for men or a nunnery for women, had its church, which was the private chapel of the house, and not open to the public. In the course of years these private chapels were built as huge churches, much larger than the parish church. Even now you may see standing close to a big college church a much smaller parish church; as, for example, St. Margaret's Church, which stands by the side of Westminster Abbey. As more land came into the possession of these religious houses, the monks had more business with the outside world; for, as landlords, they had to see that their lands were turned to good account, and cultivated according to the notions of the day.

The monasteries, especially in their early days, were great centres of good and useful work. Those who founded them, or gave them lands, did so because they felt they were doing excellent service for the people, and they wanted to have a share in the work, and to be remembered in the prayers of the monks. Founders of religious houses believed that they were getting something worth having in return for the lands which they gave.

In the wild times of the Danish invasions the monasteries were looked upon as places of safety for the weak and helpless. But they were not always safe places. Sometimes, when the country was in a disturbed state, people would send their valuables to the nearest monastery. In time the Danes got to know of this, and many a religious house was attacked and sacked by them on account of the tales they had heard of the marvellous wealth hidden there.

A story is told of a worthy person living near St. Alban's monastery at a time when a visit from marauding Danes was expected. One market-day he sent a number of heavy iron-bound chests, guarded by armed men, through the market to the monastery. Everybody, of course, turned to look, and talked about the affair. As a matter of fact the chests only contained stones; the treasure was carefully hidden somewhere else, till all danger was thought to be over. That plan was used to put the Danes "off the scent" as we should say.

All the land that did not go with the tuns and vills in early days was apparently regarded as belonging to the people, and was called the folk-land. There was a great deal of this unoccupied land, and it was not regarded at the time as being of much use to anybody. The king came to be regarded as the custodian or guardian of these folk-lands. Little by little they became the property of the king, until practically he could do what he pleased with them. It was from these folk-lands—which in early times were probably scraps of land which nobody thought to be worth very much, since the nearest vills or tuns had never taken them in—that kings gave land to bishoprics and monasteries. By and by these rough lands became very valuable; but in most cases it was the labour, the skill, and the brains of the monks in the early days which turned the waste lands into fruitful fields.

Consecration of a Saxon Church, from an ancient manuscript of Caedmon's Poems

CHAPTER XV

Later Saxon Times

Every old town and village has got its oldest house, of course. You will most likely have heard people trying to be funny about it, and saying they think it must have been built in the year One. There is, we may pretty safely say, no house now standing exactly as it was in the days of King Cnut and the later Saxon times. But even yet there are some buildings standing, and still in use, which have certain parts which were erected in those times. These buildings are mostly churches, and in various parts of the country, indeed in almost every county, something belonging to this age can be pointed out.

Churches built of stone in those days had very thick walls with very small windows. The east end of the chancel was usually semicircular, forming an apse. The wall between the chancel and the nave was pierced by a narrow, low, round-headed arch. Most of the windows had plain, round-headed arches, and in some of them, dividing the opening into two parts or "lights", were stone pillars with bulging stems. Some of the doorways had triangular heads, others had round heads. There are some very curious bits of sculpture over some of these doorways. The meaning of them was quite plain, no doubt, to the people who carved them, but they are very difficult for us to understand. They represent the ideas which the Saxons had of good and evil, and of the strife continually going on between them.

King Edward the Confessor had been brought up in Normandy, where church-building was in advance of anything in England. He encouraged Norman ideas in building, as well as in other directions, and so prepared the way for the coming of the Normans. Some parts of the buildings connected with Westminster Abbey were built at that time.

We do not know much of Saxon castles, though the Saxons had their strongholds and fortified places.

The houses in which the people lived were most of them in those days built of wood. There was not much difference, except in size, between the house of the king, the thane, and the villein. There was the hearth, on which was the fire; and the room or hall in which it was placed was the chief building, close to which, very gradually, other buildings arose. Apparently the buildings had a framework of timber, filled in with wood wattled together like hurdles. In the more important buildings stone gradually came into use.

The monasteries and convents each had the buildings in which the monks lived grouped round the church. After the Danish wars the buildings improved, stone taking the place of wood.

Even in the towns wood was chiefly used for the ordinary houses; though, as we should expect, stone was used in the more important buildings and in the wall round the town.

What we understand by comfort in a house was absent. There was the fire on the hearth in the middle of the floor; in this room the people of the house, from the highest to the lowest, had their meals; and there, on the floor, most of them slept at night. Cooking was done almost entirely in the open air.

Saxon Doorway, Earl's Barton, Northampton

CHAPTER XVI

In Norman Times

When Duke William of Normandy became King of England, the power of the Crown was greater than it had ever been before.   All the old folk-land had become king's land.   Many knights had followed Duke William from Normandy into England, and expected to be provided for by their leader.   The lands belonging to King Harold, and those of the Saxon eorls who had died fighting at Senlac, King William regarded as his own.   These he granted to his followers, on condition that they acknowledged him as their overlord, and followed him in war when required.   This was a stricter condition than had ever before been required in England.   The Normans were used to it, and it did not seem at all strange to them.

Neither was it so very strange to the Saxon nobles and thanes.   Most of them were allowed to keep their estates if they took the oath of allegiance to the king as the Normans did.   Of course they grumbled: it was only natural that they should do so; but if they did not acknowledge the king in this way they were looked upon as rebels, and lost their lands.

King William was very careful, in the grants which he made, not to put too much power into the hands of his nobles.   The old vills of Saxon times were now pretty generally called manors.   When the king granted land, it was not given in huge slices—whole counties, halves, and quarters of counties—to this great follower of his or to that one.   Between the old vills, or manors, there were often wide stretches of the king's own land, the old folk-land.   If he had granted to a Norman knight a quarter of a county or so, he would have been giving away much of his own land. Besides that, the king did not mean his followers to become too powerful. He granted the land in separate manors. It is quite true that in every county we can, so to speak, put our finger on some Norman knight who came over with William I, and say that he got the lion's share of the manors in that county. Thus in Hampshire there was Hugh de Port, and in Hertfordshire Eustace de Boulogne. But their manors did not all lie side by side, nor were they conveniently close together. Just as a villein's holding was spread out in various fields, so the manors, or fiefs, which a knight held under King William were often scattered over various counties.

At the time of the Conquest a very large number of manors belonged to bishoprics and monasteries. Now the Normans were a Christian race. The Norman Conquest was not like the Saxon or the Danish Conquest —a rush of heathen, bent on plunder and bloodshed. Bitter as the strife was, it was not as bad as those invasions had been. There was something which the Normans and the later Saxons both respected, and that was their religion. The Normans were a particularly religious and devout people, stern and cruel as they were. The lands of the Church and of the monasteries were not interfered with to any extent. King William, however, took care that they were in the hands of people whom he could trust.

The story is told that the Saxon abbot, Frederick of St. Alban's, who did not love the Normans, once remarked to King William that he owed his easy conquest of England to the fact that so many of the manors were held by monks and clergy, who could not and would not bring out their men to fight.

The king replied that that must be mended; for enemies might again invade the land, and he must have men whom he could depend upon to meet the foe.   At that time a great tract of land between St. Albans and London belonged to the Abbey, and the abbot allowed Saxon outlaws to infest it, who were a great nuisance to the Normans.   As the land had been given by former kings, the king at once took half of it back again, in order to clear out the outlaws.   Abbot Frederick had said too much.   He fled away to the Camp of Refuge at Ely, and King William would only accept as abbot a Norman and a friend of his—Paul de Caen.   That was a very good appointment for St. Albans.   The great tower of the Abbey Church, still standing, was built by him—more than eight centuries ago.

CHAPTER XVII

In Norman Times (*Cont.*)

The king, then, granted manors to his followers, and to such Saxon eorls and thanes as were willing to hold their lands on the same conditions as the Normans.   If they objected, as from time to time a good many of them did, they had to go.

Now, though every manor had a lord, where the lord held many manors it was quite impossible for him to be living in the manor-house of each of them, and looking after his estate himself.   He could, if he chose, let out some portions of these manors to a man beneath him in rank, on exactly the same conditions as the king had granted to him.   The man must swear to be his vassal, and appear, when required, with his proper number of men, to fight his lord's battles.   He, in his turn, might let parts of the lands to others under him.

By this means the king could command a pretty large army.   He would summon his great vassals, they would summon their vassals, each of whom would in turn summon his followers; and so from every manor men would be called to fight. It was something like the old nursery tale: "The fire began to burn the stick; the stick began to beat the dog; the dog began to worry the pig; and so the pig began to get over the stile".

If the lord was not living in the manor-house there was someone there to represent him and to look after his interests. In scores of manors the people never set eyes on their overlord; but they felt the grip of his power through the steward of the manor. Now, though the steward could not go against the customs of the manor openly, there were many ways in which he could make himself very disagreeable to the people under his care. He was there to grind what he could out of the tenants for the lord, and he took care to grind for himself too. It seems to have been quite an understood thing that he was to get what he could out of the manor for himself, so that very often villeins and tenants had anything but an easy, pleasant life.

The Norman Conquest did not interfere with the customs of the manors, and the life of an ordinary manor went on very much the same in King William's reign as it had done under King Edward the Confessor. About twenty years after King William I had come to the throne, that great survey, recorded in Domesday Book, was made. Learned men who have studied the Domesday Book closely have discovered many things connected with the life of people in England at this period. We can even see what parts of the country suffered by opposing King William, and which districts had submitted quietly to him.

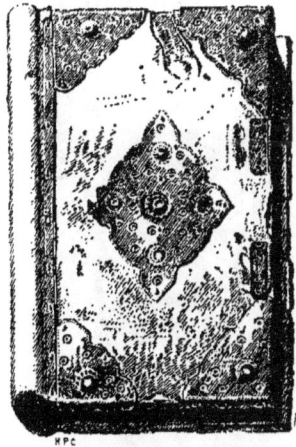

Domesday Book. From the original in the Public Record Office, London. (⅛ *original size.*)

CHAPTER XVIII

In Norman Times: The Churches

When we speak of Norman times we must bear in mind that they lasted for over one hundred and thirty years—say from 1066 to 1200. That period covers a good many years, and consequently a good many changes took place. Now this period is marked by a particular style of architecture known as Norman or Twelfth Century.

With the coming of William the Conqueror to England began a great period of building in this country. There was what we may almost call a "great rage" for founding or establishing religious houses and churches, and for building castles. All the religious houses have gone, and nearly all the castles, but in their ruins we can see specimens of Norman work. In a large number of old churches we can see very good examples of this style. In Hampshire especially there is scarcely one old church, even in the most out-of-the-way village, which has not some Norman work to show.

You will expect to find that the style of building altered somewhat during that long time. In the beginning it was very plain, but gradually it became more ornamental. At first there were plain, round-headed arches and heavy stone pillars, with boldly cut caps to them. But in the time of King Henry II, and later, we find the mouldings of the arches, and the caps of the pillars, ornamented more and more with bold carvings. There is a vast difference between the plain, almost ugly,

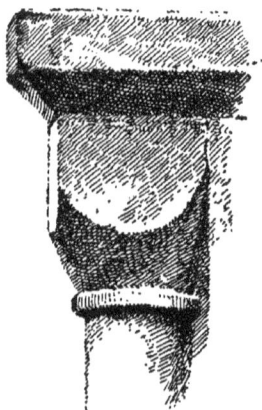

Norman Capital, Buckland
Church, Berks

CHOIR OF CANTERBURY CATHEDRAL

The Transition work is to be seen especially in the columns and arches on either side of the choir

[See page 57]

.

Norman work, in St. Alban's Cathedral, which was begun about the year 1077, and the Norman work which can be seen in Durham Cathedral, or the west door of Rochester Cathedral. The St. Albans builders had no stone at hand to speak of, but any amount of Roman tiles from the ruins of Verulam. They could not build anything very ornamental, but they could and did build something vast and imposing. In most of the cathedrals there are still to be seen very fine specimens of later Norman work.

Norman Capital, Hanney Church, Berks

We see, towards the end of the period, from the way in which the Norman arches were used to intersect each other and form two pointed arches within a round-headed arch, that a change in style was showing itself. Towards the end of Norman times, in the reigns of Richard I and John, we reach what architects call the Transition Period, when the Norman style was gradually changing into the Early English or Pointed Style. The choir of Canterbury Cathedral is one of the best-known specimens of this Transition Period. Just as changes took place in the style of the buildings, so, too, the life of the nation changed. All the changes were not improvements; some, indeed, were changes for the worse.

Norman Capital, St. Bartholomew's Priory Church, London

CHAPTER XIX

Castles

The passion for building castles in England had begun before the Norman Conquest; but during the Norman period a great many castles (about eleven hundred, it is said) were built in various parts of the country. They were not all of the same size, strength, or importance. Some were royal castles, belonging to the king, who placed each one in charge of a constable or warden. These were necessary for the defence of the country. We should expect to find important castles, for instance, at such places as Carlisle, Ludlow, Gloucester, Dover, and London. We can, too, trace lines of castles along the Scottish and Welsh borders; and there were no fewer than twenty-five in the county of Monmouth alone.

Many castles were placed on the sites of Saxon strongholds, and of strongholds dating from still earlier times. Others were built where the overlord thought they would be of service to him in protecting his interests and keeping his tenants in order. So it often came to pass that the castles were built close to, or in the very heart of, a town or city. Frequently the castle was at once the protection and the terror of the neighbourhood.

It is curious to note that some of the greatest castle-builders of the time were bishops. There was Bishop Gundulph of Rochester, who built the Keep of Rochester Castle and the White Tower in the Tower of London. There was Bishop Henry de Blois of Winchester, who built a number of castles on lands belonging to his bishopric. Strange as it may seem to us that bishops should be great rulers and leaders of armies, it did not strike the people of those days as at all extraordinary or improper. A bishop was as much a ruler as the king, and had territories to look after and keep in order. In those days he was quite as able to carry out these duties as the boldest baron

Rochester Castle: The Keep

Rochester Castle was built by Bishop Gundulf between 1077 and 1108, under the order of William Rufus. The magnificent Keep (70 feet square and 104 feet high) was added about 1126.

of them all, and could give and take hard knocks with the best of them.

The great castle-builders had no love for the traders in towns and cities; indeed they looked down on that class. But they found them very useful. Towns attracted traders by land and by water; and every town, every bridge, and every ferry belonged to some lord or other. No goods could be brought into or taken from a town, or carried across bridge or ferry, without paying toll and custom to the overlord. But he had certain duties to perform in return, in protecting the town and its trade; and the better the protection the more traders came to pay toll, and the better it was for everybody concerned.

So we find, near many of our ancient towns and cities, a castle, or its ruins—or perhaps only the site is left—where the lord of the town kept a number of men to protect the town and district, even when he was not there himself.

If there was no love lost between the lord of the castle and the townsmen, there was still less between the latter and the soldiers. The soldiers were inclined to take liberties, and to be insolent and oppressive. As they had it in their power to "make trouble", if not kept in good-humour, the townsmen put up with much for the sake of peace and quietness.

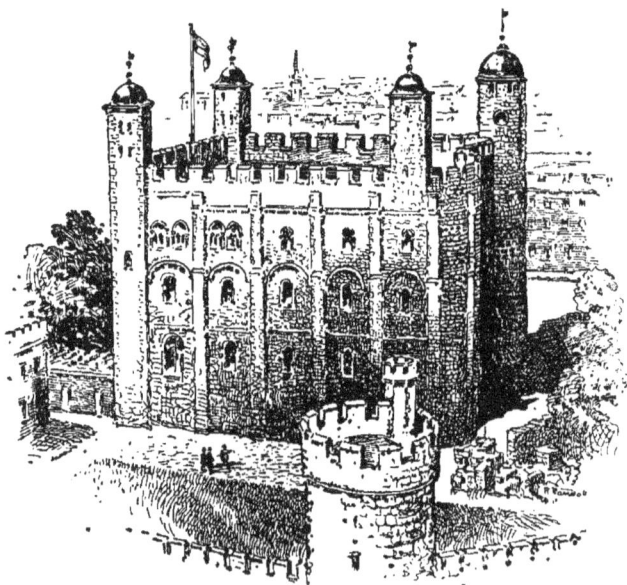

The White Tower, Tower of London, built by Gundulf, Bishop of Rochester, 1078. The exterior was restored by Wren, but within the Norman work is little altered

CHAPTER XX

Castles and Towns

However useful a castle might be in protecting the overlord's tenants and property, the sense of security was always a great temptation to quarrel with other lords. With strong kings, like William I and Henry I, the danger of disorder was not so great, as these monarchs knew how to keep their great barons in check. But in the time of King Stephen, during the long years of civil war, the barons were divided into two parties, and each castle became a centre of strife.

The baron in his castle had his men to keep. These he did not pay in regular wages. He fed, clothed, and armed them after a fashion; and, to give them something to do, would rake up some old grievance with a neighbouring baron, make an attack upon his property, and let his men plunder, burn, and kill to their hearts' content. Then the other baron would retaliate.

It is easy to see that the conditions of life in England were most unsettled in the reign of King Stephen. There was no safety in town or village, and the dwellers on the manors must have suffered most severely. Their own lord would send and gather in all their store to victual his castle from time to time: his enemy would send *his* men to seize what they could. It made very little real difference to the villeins which side won; *they* suffered, as they were heavily oppressed by both parties. Their own lord expected his dues just the same, war or no war, famine or no famine, whether he or his enemy had carried off the best part of the corn and cattle or not; and he would take his pick of the men on his manors to fill the places of his men-at-arms who had been put out of action.

Many of the barons became little better than monsters of cruelty, and their castles " nests of devils and dens of thieves ". One of the very worst of these was Geoffrey de Mandeville, who had large estates in Essex and Hertfordshire. His castle of Anstey, in Hertfordshire, was a den of fearful wickedness. He and his men neither feared God nor regarded man; nothing was sacred to them—they spared neither church nor monastery, town nor village.

Dreadful tales are still told of the cruel deeds done in the deep dungeons of nearly all these old castles by the "bold bad barons" of the time of King Stephen.

When Henry II became king he put a stop to these disorders, and large numbers of the castles were pulled down; but the evils they had caused lived long after, and were the source of much trouble.

It is said that "Everything comes to those who know how to wait", and the townsmen, under the rule of a great lord, knew how to wait. Great as the lord of the town was, whether he was baron, bishop, or the king himself, he could not do without the town—and the town knew it. People were sometimes short of ready money in those days just at the very time when they needed it most urgently.

You will remember that the Crusades began in the reign of King William II. Now and again the crusading "fever" took hold of some of these Norman barons, and many wanted to go to fight the Turk—especially when there was not much fighting going on at home. But crusading was a costly business, and of course there was a good deal of rivalry between these crusading knights as to who could raise the best-furnished troop of men. The baron would be glad to get together as much money as he could. So the chance came to many a town to advance money to their lord. He, in return, would grant to the town the right to collect the tolls and

customs payable to him for a term of years ; or perhaps
on condition that they allowed him so much every year
out of the tolls collected.

Bishops, too, were often in urgent need of money, for
there were many calls upon them. The monasteries
were, at this period, beginning to do so much expensive
building, that often they, too, were glad to get money

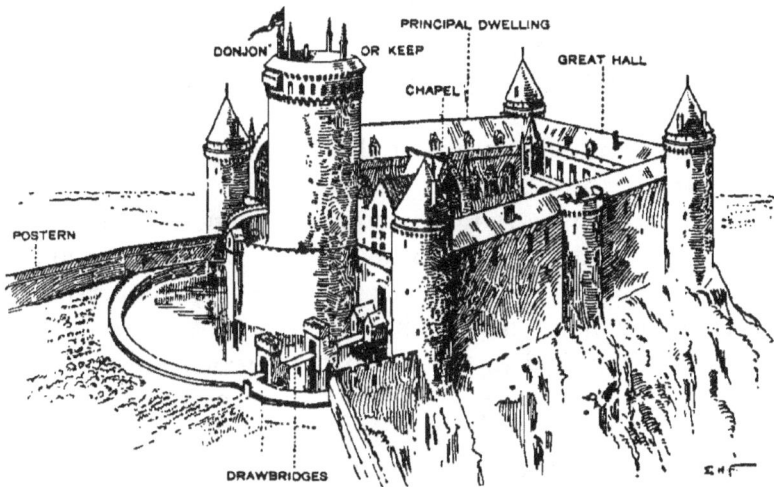

Norman Castle (based on that of Coucy in the north of France). Coucy
(*built between 1230–1242*) *was a magnificent example of a feudal fortress. The " keep " was round instead of rectangular.*

by granting to the townsmen privileges for which they
were willing to pay.

Then there were other towns, not depending so closely
on a baron or bishop or monastery, which wanted to
gain similar privileges of levying toll and custom.
These would petition the king for the right to be given
to them too, to levy dues, in return for a large sum of
money paid down, or for a yearly payment to the king.

The towns were becoming strong, and they gained
considerable rights during this Norman period. As

far back as the time of King Cnut we find, in some districts, towns banding themselves together to protect their trade and interests. This was the case with Leicester, Nottingham, Derby, Stamford, and Lincoln.

CHAPTER XXI

In Norman Times: The Monasteries

The hundred years after the Norman Conquest was a great period of building. It was a time for establishing or *founding* new religious houses. Something like three hundred and ninety-eight such houses were opened during this period, so that they played a very important part in the history of the times. The Normans were not very much interested in the English religious houses which they found already established here. In fact, a good many of them, since the times of the Danish invasion, two hundred years before, had got into very bad order, and were in need of reform. Little by little, as Norman bishops and abbots were appointed over these Saxon religious houses, reforms did take place, but not always very easily or quietly.

At the time of the Conquest the religious houses in Normandy were in a far better state than those in England. Their members lived better lives, did better work, and set a much better example of godly living and working. There were several new orders or societies of monks, which had their head-quarters on the continent of Europe. These interested King William's companions more than the old English monasteries, because they and their fathers had helped to establish them.

So we find, as the Normans received lands here in England, and founded religious houses, most of them were connected with the monasteries across the sea, and were ruled by abbots who lived across the sea. Such branch houses were generally called priories, and the kings and barons who founded them gave them manors and parts of manors, sometimes taking them from the older Saxon monasteries and cathedrals.[1]

Then, too, there were the old Saxon houses, St. Alban's

Ruins of Furness Abbey

Built about sixty years after the Norman Conquest. Much of it was destroyed in the time of Henry VIII.

Abbey, Westminster Abbey, and Glastonbury Abbey: they were reformed and improved, and to them, too, lands were given in various parts of the country, often far away from the mother house. Thus St. Alban's Monastery had important lands in the neighbourhood of the River Tyne, and a daughter house was opened there called Tynemouth Priory. So, you see, there were two kinds of priories in England: one class attached to English religious houses, and the other to Norman or foreign

[1] The Cistercian houses here in England, however, were always known as *abbeys*, though Citeaux, their head-quarters, was in France.

religious houses.   In time the foreign priories received
the name of alien priories.

In time a good deal of ill-feeling arose towards these
alien priories, as the people in England did not like so
much money going out of the country, especially in war
times.   King John was the first king to seize these
priories when he fell out with France.   Later, King
Edward I, in 1295, seized the property of about one
hundred of the alien priories in various parts of England
to help to pay his war expenses.   There were several of
these alien houses in the Isle of Wight, and, thinking
that the monks might be aiding his enemies across the
English Channel, the king sent the monks to other
houses on the mainland, a long way away from the coast,
to keep them out of mischief.   When the war was over,
the property was restored to these priories, and the monks
returned to them.   This kind of thing happened over and
over again.

All these religious houses had some interest in the
land, and all of them, to a greater or lesser degree, were
landlords.   In some cases the lands given to them were
manors which had been managed and tilled in the same
way for hundreds of years.   The only change was that
the lord of the manor might be a society or religious
house instead of a baron.   Each of the manors had its
steward, its villeins, and so forth, like any other in the
land.   But a good deal of the land given to these new
religious houses had never been occupied before.

Though some of the monasteries, like St. Alban's and
St. Edmund's Bury, were in towns, there were others,
especially those founded in these Norman times, far
away from towns, in pathless woods or deep dales, like
Rievaulx, in Yorkshire.   Others, like Ramsey and
Thorney, were in lonely fens and marshes.   Here the
monks themselves set to work, as in the earlier days,
and tilled the ground, keeping up their regular services

Foundation of a Minster

From a thirteenth-century drawing in the British Museum.

in their little churches most carefully — praying and working. Gradually their lands improved; other lands came to them; more labour was needed; and so, little by little, tenants took holdings on their lands, and farmed them for the "house", on much the same conditions as in the older manors.

We find that in many of the monasteries attention was given to other occupations besides agriculture. Some, especially those in towns, like St. Alban's, became in this period great seats of learning. All of them copied the books they used, and some of them were particularly famed for their writing and illuminating. In fact, they were the book-producers of the age, and very little of the work of learned ancient scholars could have come down to us had it not been for the careful, painstaking work of simple monks quite unknown to history.

Some of the abbeys in the west of England, like Bath Abbey, had a good deal to do with opening up the wool trade, which in the Middle Ages became the staple trade of the south and west of England. Flaxley Abbey, in

Gloucestershire, developed iron-smelting.   The iron
mines in Furness were developed there by the monks,
and also in the neighbouring Walney Isle, off the Lan-
cashire coast.   At Rievaulx, in Yorkshire, there were
ironworks near the abbey, and at Malvern Priory there
was ornamental tile-making carried on, specimens of the
work done there remaining in a good many Worcester-
shire churches still.   Monks gave great attention to their
gardens, and were very clever in fish culture; and in
many simple, homely ways they showed men how to
develop the natural resources of the land.

In the monasteries men could quietly think and work,
and use the talents they had, without being called away
to fight or do the unskilled work of the world.   In these
early times there were no other places where men could
lead quiet, thoughtful lives, and "think things out", and
then put them into practice.   The men in the monasteries were not all equally good or religious or clever,
but the work done in and through these old institutions
was most important and most valuable to the country.

Bath Abbey.   Founded 676; rebuilt in the Perpendicular style, 1499

CHAPTER XXII

Early Houses

When we go from a big modern manufacturing town into an old town or village, we cannot help noticing the old buildings, the ancient churches, the old town hall, the alms-houses, and the old houses with their plastered fronts, tiled roofs, and huge chimney-stacks.

As years go by, the number of these old houses gets less and less. In the course of time, many of the smaller ones especially, which have been neglected and allowed to fall into bad repair, become dangerous to live in. The sanitary inspector and the medical officer of health condemn them as unfit for human habitation, and the houses are shut up. Then, perhaps, they stand empty for some years; mischievous boys throw stones and break the glass left in the queer little windows; bill-posters paste notices of all kinds on the doors, walls, and window-shutters; holes are knocked in the plaster, bits of the woodwork are torn away, chalk-marks are scrawled on the walls, and the buildings very shortly look disgracefully untidy. Then some day the "house-breaker" appears on the scene, and the houses, which have stood for centuries, are cleared away, and modern buildings take their places.

Thoughtful people who know something of the history of the town or village are always sorry to see old buildings disappear; because there is much to be learned from them, and they help us to recall many things of great value and importance which we very easily lose sight of.

But, old as the houses in our streets and villages are, there are very few of them which date back more than three hundred or three hundred and fifty years. Most of them only date back to the time of Queen Elizabeth—the latter part of the sixteenth century.

There are, however, a number of fine old houses which have work in them of the thirteenth and four-teenth centuries, and some people can point out to you traces of work in some old houses of an earlier date than that. There is at Lincoln, for instance, a fine old stone house called "the Jew's House", which was built late in the twelfth century. Of course, since it was built, it has, from time to time, been altered to suit the needs and the fancies of the various folk who have lived in it. But stone houses for ordinary people, both in towns and villages, were very rare then—wood was the common material. Of course in parts of the country where stone was plentiful, and wood scarce, stone would be very largely used. For instance, amongst the Cotswolds stone has always been the handiest material for building walls, and for covering roofs. In the course of centuries much of this stone has been used over and over again, and has been "weathered" into a very beautiful tone, such as only time can give. Such old buildings are much loved and appreciated by folk who have an eye to see the beauty of colouring.

Nowadays, both in town and country, houses are commonly "bunches of bricks". The Romans knew how to make bricks or tiles, and in places near old Roman cities Roman tile is still to be seen, which has been used up over and over again in the walls of old buildings. The big tower of St. Alban's Cathedral is built of Roman tiles which had been used centuries before in the walls of Roman houses in Verulamium.[1] That tower has been standing as it is now for over eight hundred years.

But in Saxon times the *art* of brick-making was lost, and Saxons and Normans, it appears, were quite

[1] Commonly called Verulam, but Verulamium was its Roman name.

ignorant of it. There is an old brick house—Little Wenham Hall, in Suffolk—which is believed to have been built in the latter part of the thirteenth century. That is the oldest brick house in England. In the fifteenth century the art of brick-making had been rediscovered, and it seems to have been imported from Flanders. We find specimens of such brickwork in places near the east coast, and this old brickwork is more pleasing to the eye than our modern brick. Here, again, time has done its work in beautifying. The old palace at Hatfield is one of the brick buildings of this period; but brick did not come much into use until quite a century later. In the county of Middlesex, where there is found clay which is very suitable for brick-making, the art was not used to any great extent till the time of King James I. After the Great Fire of London, in the year 1666, there was a great demand for bricks, and the use of that material has quite changed the character of the houses in our towns and villages.

The Jew's House, Lincoln

CHAPTER XXIII

Early Houses (*Cont.*)

For many centuries the houses of the villeins and cottiers did not alter very much in their general plan. You will remember that in those old pit-dwellings the hearth and its fire were the centre of the home. The room, or space round the fire, gradually became larger, especially in the houses of the thanes and eorls, till we get the hall, with the hearth in the middle and the hole in the roof to let out the smoke.

All through the later Saxon and Danish times, and in the Norman period, the hall was the most important part of the house. As the years went on, and the style of building altered, the walls, the windows, and the roof became more beautiful and ornamental, becoming most magnificent in the fourteenth century, or Decorated Period. Gradually other buildings were added to the hall for comfort and convenience.

So far as we know, the house or hut of the villein was a very simple affair before the time of the Norman Conquest. Two pairs of poles were set up, sloped, and joined at the top, and connected by a ridge pole as shown in the illustration. The space between was then filled in by other poles and wattle-work. This was plastered with clay, and covered with turf or rough thatch. There seems to have been a pretty regular length for this building, which was long enough to take four stalls for oxen. That required about sixteen feet and was called a "bay". The villein

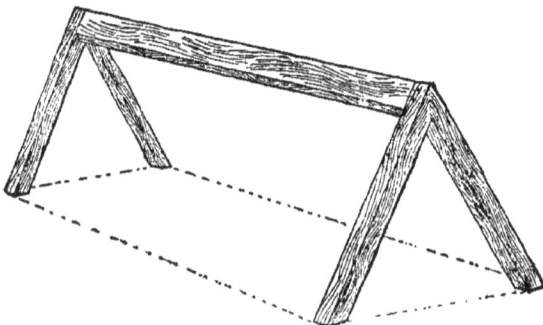

THE OLD PALACE, HATFIELD

[See page 93]

and his oxen were all housed under one roof at first. When another bay was added, the size of the house was doubled, and so on. In the course of time the houses were improved; side walls were raised of wood framing, and the sides were filled in with wattle and covered with clay.

As the years went on, these houses or huts grew out of date, and were replaced by others in much the same style, but gradually improving in comfort and workmanship. In the villages there was not much alteration down to the fourteenth century. When a house in a manor or village was pulled down, and was to be rebuilt, the manor court kept a sharp eye upon the building operations to see that the new walls did not encroach upon the highway, or upon the lord's land. No addition could be made to the house without the consent of the overlord. Customs in the villages changed very, very slowly, and so it is that, though the houses in out-of-the-way villages have been rebuilt over and over again, there are many lath-and-plaster houses standing now round village greens, built between two and three hundred years ago, on old foundations which date back to Saxon times.

We gave as an instance on p. 26 the case of Exton, in Rutland. There the houses even to-day, in spite of the fact that they have often been rebuilt and somewhat modified in the course of centuries, occupy the same sites as they did in Saxon times. No one would dream of laying out a village on those lines to-day, and in the great changes which we know are greatly needed in housing all over the country, and which are bound to affect every village in the land more or less and to change the whole aspect of these old-world villages, it will be well if some *specimens*, at least, can be preserved to us, so that those yet to come may be able to see how our ancestors for many generations were housed. But

Old House, Cleveland, Yorkshire

The remains of a common type of rural dwelling in the Middle Ages.   The wooden frame which supported the steep-pitched roof can be seen.

the health of the people will have to be safeguarded most carefully, and much of that which is old will have to give place to that which is new.

So for many hundreds of years an ordinary village house was, to our way of thinking, a very wretched, comfortless place.   Even as late as the time of Queen Elizabeth a countryman's house is thus described :—

> " Of one bay's breadth, God wot, a silly cote,
> Whose thatchèd spars are furred with sluttish soote
> A whole inch thick, shining like blackmoor's brows
> Through smoke that down the headlesse barrel blows.
> At his bed's feete feaden[1] his stallèd teame,
> His swine beneath, his pullen[2] o'er the beam."

    [1] *feaden*, that is, feed.   [2] *pullen*, that is, poultry.

CHAPTER XXIV

Early Town Houses

Houses in towns have been more frequently rebuilt and altered in various ways than those in the villages. The chief material used in building was wood, as it was in the villages, and one of the great dangers in the Middle Ages was that of fire. In the towns this danger was greater than in the villages, and fires happened more frequently.

The leading men in a town had more money to spend, and the increase of business, or a desire for change, led them to improve their houses. It was easier for a wealthy townsman to get leave from the " corporation ", or guild which ruled the town, to rebuild his house than it was for the villein in the village to get the leave of the manor court.

The thirteenth, fourteenth, and fifteenth centuries all saw a great growth in architecture; they were the Early English, the Decorated, and the Perpendicular Periods of architecture. In most of the old churches, and in many of the old mansions, we have specimens of all these periods; but not very many of the town houses founded in the Middle Ages, and still standing, are much earlier than the fifteenth century. In that age there was a great development of woodwork, and there is hardly one old town which has not some woodwork of that time in some of its old houses.

The rich and prosperous townsman rebuilt his house according to the fashion of his time; but through all the three centuries the general arrangements of the dwelling-house did not alter very much.

In some parts of London, and in many country towns, you can see that some of the very old-fashioned shops in the main street are reached from the pavement by a little flight of steps. Below the shop there is a big light cellar, and the small boy or girl who wants to look in at the shop window has to "tiptoe" very much in order to do so. Now, that arrangement is just a little relic of the old town house of the Middle Ages.

The house was usually quite narrow, and had a gable facing the street. It was built over a cellar of stone, often arched and vaulted very much like a church. There were steps from the street down to the cellar, and these steps had to be protected, or accidents were certain to happen to careless foot-passengers. Then, too, there were steps up to the room over the cellar, which formed the shop and workroom in one. The front of the shop would be open, like a stall, and there would probably be a passage through to the back of the house.

Above the shop would be another room or rooms, over which, in the open space under the roof, was the great attic running through the house. This attic was often kept as a store-room, and goods were hoisted from the street by a crane; but in later times it would be formed most likely into little sleeping-rooms, very small, very, dark, and very unhealthy. Very often they led one into the other, and had no windows or means of proper ventilation.

Most of the work would be done in the shop, where the master, his workmen, and apprentices all did their share. The apprentices would sleep in the shop at night, and very probably the workmen as well. It was quite a usual thing for all the establishment to work and live and sleep on the premises. The rooms occupied by the master and his family at first were few in number; separate bedrooms only came into use very gradually indeed.

The walls of the house above the cellar were usually of wood, and the front towards the street was often

CHAS WADE

Shop of the Middle Ages now standing in Foregate Street, Chester

skilfully and beautifully carved. In some English counties still there are very fine specimens of these old town houses; those at Chester, Shrewsbury, and Ludlow, for instance, are famed all over the world.

We must not suppose that all the houses were equally splendid, or equally well built; there was then, no doubt, bad building as well as good. In fact there must have been some very careless building in early days, and especially so in Norman times. It is a curious fact that almost every big Norman church tower tumbled down because it was badly built, even though Norman work looked very massive and substantial, and was very imposing.

Merchants and wealthy tradesmen took great pride in

their houses, and the woodwork and furniture in them were splendid. Kings and nobles were no better housed than these wealthy townsmen, nor did they have more of the comforts of life.

But the poor! There were always the poor and the outcast in every town; but they did not exist in the enormous numbers of later years, or of the present day. Their wretched little hovels were huddled together in close alleys, and life in them must have been very cheerless and unwholesome. It was, however, *somebody's* business to look after them. The religious houses, the churches, the colleges, all did their part in distributing food at their gates daily. Many wealthy people, both nobles and citizens, did likewise, and to give alms to the poor was a work of charity which no self-respecting citizen thought of shirking. Then, too, the guild or corporation kept a sharp look-out upon the poor; strangers were turned out of the town, and the people punished who had taken them into their houses without having the consent of the town authorities. In old town records we often come across instances of people being punished for "harbouring inmates".

A Cradle of the Fourteenth Century now in a London Museum

CHAPTER XXV

Life in the Towns of the Middle Ages

Disease was one of the great dangers always lurking in a town. Plague of some kind or other was never very far away, and it frequently made its presence felt. People had not realized the sinfulness of dirt.

The best-drained buildings were the monasteries and colleges. Near the ruins of every big monastery, from time to time, underground passages have been discovered, many of them big enough for a man to walk along upright, and leading nobody knows where. When these were found, people shook their heads and said: "Ah, those old monks; you don't know what they were up to! They made these secret passages, going for miles and miles underground, so that they might get in and out of the monastery, and be up to all sorts of mischief, without anyone being the wiser."

Many wonderful tales have been told about these underground passages; but, as a matter of fact, most, if not all of them, have turned out to be sewers, which the monks made from their monasteries to a watercourse some distance away, so that the sewage might be safely got rid of. The monks were usually in advance of the townsmen of those days in sanitary matters. No doubt a sanitary engineer of the present day would be able to point out how much better the drainage-works could have been carried out; but the monks set an example in this matter which, bit by bit, the rest of the nation began to follow.

The chief streets of the town and the market-place were paved with huge lumps of stone, sloping towards the middle of the street from the houses on each side of the way, a gutter or "denter" running down the middle. All sorts of filth were flung into the gutter, for there were no drains from the houses in early days. When a heavy shower of rain fell, the water flushed the gutter more or less. If the street happened to be pretty level, the gutter, or denter, was just an open sewer all the year round; and it did its deadly work in poisoning the worthy citizens, though they did not realize it. Those towns were the best drained which were perched on a steep slope, so that the contents of the gutter found their way speedily to the nearest water-course. By that means they got rid of *some* of the filth, but they did not improve the watercourse.

There were no great manufacturing towns in those days. Most of the ordinary articles used by the towns-folk were manufactured in the town itself, and much of the work went on in the open air. The butcher killed his animals in the street, before his shop, and that added to the horrors and stenches of the gutter. But then all the butchers in a town were located in one part of it. Even now most old towns have got a Shambles, or Butchers' Row, or Butchery Street, or place of similar name, near the market-place. Other trades had their own parts of the town, where they made and sold their goods. Cordwinder Street or Shoe-makers' Row are still common street names. The smith and the armourer did much of their work out in the open street; the joiner put together there any big piece of woodwork which he had in hand; the wheel-wright "shut" his tyres; the chandler melted fat and made candles. The streets of the town must have been very noisy and very "smelly".

There were no footways for passengers. Wagons, drays, and wheel-barrows there were, but carriages had hardly been invented, and coaches and light-wheeled vehicles had not been dreamt of. Travellers mostly went on horses or mules.

The Shambles, York; a street that preserves its narrow, mediæval character

No doubt the tradesmen were expected to clear up the mess they made in front of their houses, and the apprentices had to sweep up. But that usually meant only drawing the rubbish together to the great refuse-heap close to the house, which the fowls and the pigs, to say nothing of the children, speedily managed to scatter. Now and then the town authorities would wake up and make a fuss, and these heaps would be carted away to a spot outside the town; but usually the street was looked upon as the handiest place into which to fling any refuse from the houses. However clean the citizens' houses might be inside, and however richly ornamented the woodwork and the furniture, plague and pestilence were always very near.

Still, though many persons died, and were buried close by in the little churchyard, where for hundreds of years the dead had been buried, people lived, and throve, and did good work. For one thing, they lived a great deal in the open air, and they were not so much afraid of draughts in their houses as we are.

The water-supply of a town was a very important matter. Here, again, the monasteries and colleges frequently led the way, and showed how water might be brought by pipes from a distant spring. It was not an uncommon thing for water to be brought in this way to a "conduit" in the market-place, whence the people fetched it as they needed. Many a good wealthy citizen has performed the pious work of providing his town with a supply of water. Parts of old water-pipes, some of wood and some of lead, laid for such a purpose, have often been discovered in recent years.

Usually, however, a town had to depend upon wells for its water-supply, and water drawn from the nearest stream; and with open gutters running through the town it is very easy to see that many of these wells supplied water which, at times, could not have been pure, however bright and clear it may have looked, and it could never be relied upon as really fit for drinking purposes.

In the villages the dangers arising from want of

proper drainage and from impure water were not quite so great as in the towns. Yet even now, in this twentieth century, how to drain our villages properly, and provide them with a good water-supply, is an urgent problem in many places. For many years people have realized that the evil exists, but we have been slow to apply the right remedy because of the expense. And the nation has greatly suffered in health in consequence. We have seen that the houses in the villages were usually close together, and men had not realized that dirt is one of the greatest enemies of mankind. There are a good many people, even in our time, who see no great harm in having pigsties, refuse-heaps, and manure-heaps close to their houses.

One of the most loathsome of the diseases common in Norman times and later was leprosy. The lepers *were* kept out of the towns, but at first very little was done for them. The refuse of the markets, and the food that was so bad that it had to be carted outside the town, was thought to be good enough for them. Gradually, however, we find hospitals for lepers established. They were not what we understand by hospitals, places where sick folk could be doctored and nursed and cured; they were religious houses which poor lepers might enter, and in which they might have safe shelter, care, and attention for the rest of their sad lives. They were always built outside the walls of the towns.

Other hospitals for poor and suffering people were also established. They were not large buildings, with wards holding scores of people. They were little religious houses, each with its chapel and priests to carry on its services, providing homes for small numbers— perhaps half a dozen or a dozen. Almost every town had a number of these hospitals.

Kings, bishops, earls, and citizens all took part in this good work. Every founder expected that every day

Hospital of St. Cross, Winchester, founded 1136.   Under the archway beneath
· the tower the wayfarers "dole" is still distributed

"for ever" he and his family should be prayed for by
the inmates.   Some hospitals were "founded" or established as thank-offerings for escape from some great
danger; some to "make up" for some wrong that had
been done and could never be put right, and to show
that the founder was "really sorry"; some were built
for good reasons, others for selfish reasons.   Nowadays
we arrange fêtes and demonstration, whist drives, enter-
tainments, bazaars, sales of work, jumble sales, dances,
for our hospital funds, Red Cross funds, and orphan
funds, and we are asked to buy tickets because "it's a
good cause".   We get some enjoyment for ourselves and
help the hospital; thus, as it were, doing good and receiving good at the same time.   We need not look down
upon our ancestors as being merely selfish creatures.

CHAPTER XXVI

The Growing Power of the Towns

Back in early Saxon times we find that the inhabitants of a town were banded together to keep the peace, thus forming a society pledged to each other—the Peace or Frith Guild. It lost nearly all its *real* power in later Saxon and Norman times. But it did not actually die out, and it appears that from this Frith Guild what we now understand by a corporation took its rise. The. guild was a great power in some of the Saxon towns; only those belonging to it could trade in the town, and its members were very slow to admit outsiders to share in their privileges.

We have seen that the free, or nearly free, tuns gradually came under the power of an overlord—the king, a bishop, a baron, or a monastery, as the case might be—and very little real power was left to the guild. The overlord appointed a reeve to look after his interests, and the government of the place was in his hands. Yet the old Frith Guild seems to have regulated matters connected with the *customs* of the town, which did not interfere with the lord's rights.

When we reach Norman times we have come to a period during which the towns improved their position. The Norman Conquest led to increased trade with the Continent. The great building operations here attracted skilled workmen and craftsmen to this country. These men natu-

Seal of Guild Merchant, Gloucester, 1200.
The city gates are represented in the centre.

rally found their way to the towns rather than to the villages. They were protected and encouraged by the Norman nobles, who preferred *their* work to that of the Saxons. Although they might be foreigners, these strangers had ideas of freedom and liberty which fitted in very well with the town's ideas of self-government. Then, too, these craftsmen were bound together in trade societies or guilds, and that made them strong and worthy of consideration in the places where they settled.

A charter to a town granted and secured to it certain privileges, and a town with a charter became a borough town. The king granted a good many charters to towns during the Norman period. A town which wished to get a charter had to pay heavily for it. But it was quite worth while for the town to secure the right which a charter gave it—the right to manage its own affairs. What a town most desired was to be free from the authority of the king's officer, to choose its own port-reeve, who could preside over the court of the town, so that the town might not have to appear before the hundred court. By paying an annual rent to the king, however heavy the amount might be, the town hoped to escape from the many extra fees and taxes which the king's officers put upon it. It could then settle its own disputes, raise its own taxes as it needed them, and punish its own evil-doers.

In many cases bishops, barons, or religious houses were the overlords of districts containing important towns, and those towns managed to get charters from their overlords as other towns had from the king. By so doing they could get out of the power of the sheriff or shire-reeve. Charter or borough towns have most of them been very particular to preserve their rights and privileges.

If you live in a small country borough town, or a city,

you wiil notice that two different benches of magistrates sit in the town-hall to hear police cases; and there are two different courts of justice, though held often in the same room. There are first of all the Borough Sessions, at which the mayor of the borough presides, and which deal with cases arising in the borough, whether trifling or serious. Then, on another fixed day in the week, in the very same building, another body or bench of magistrates sits. These gentlemen usually come in from country places outside the town, and the cases brought before them have to do with the mischief done in the villages and country parishes. These magistrates have nothing at all to do with offences committed within the borough. These are the county magistrates, and their court is called the Petty Sessions, or the County Sessions.

Some offences are too grave for the borough or county magistrates to settle, and they have to be tried by a higher court of justice, which has greater powers than the Court of Petty Sessions—the Court of Quarter Sessions. The bench of this court is made up of magistrates drawn from all parts of the county, and a jury of twelve men, householders, from different parts of the county, has to be sworn to hear the evidence in the cases to be tried. The jury decides whether the man is proved to be guilty or not, when they have heard all that can be urged for and against him, and the magistrates decide what his punishment is to be, according to law.

There are some cases too grave or too complicated for the Court of Quarter Sessions to decide, and these have to stand over to the Assizes. These Assizes are held three times a year in the county town of each county, and every prisoner in the county jail must be accounted for. The court is presided over by one or more of the king's judges. These are trained lawyers, and they attend in the king's place, and are treated with much pomp and ceremony.

The sheriff of the county, properly attended, must meet the judge or judges upon arrival. Formerly when judges on circuit travelled by road from one county town to the next county town, the sheriff of the assize town to which they were travelling met them some distance from the town with a band of horsemen in quaint, old-time uniforms, armed with javelins; and in a similar way attended them for some distance out of the town when the assize was over. In most places the javelin men have disappeared, or nearly disappeared, and this guard of honour is supplied by mounted policemen. But there are a good many quaint old customs and ceremonies still observed in connection with the holding of the assizes.

Court-house of Godmanchester, Hunts

An open court in which law proceedings were conducted in the Middle Ages.

FACSIMILE OF A PORTION OF A NORMAN DOCUMENT

Part of the accounts of the sheriffs (who acted as the king's bailiffs) of London and the various counties for the year 1130-1. The portion shown refers to Middlesex, and was photographed from the original in the Public Record Office, London

.

CHAPTER XXVII

The Villages, Manors, Parishes, and Parks

We have seen that in Norman times the whole country was, so to speak, the king's. There were the great lords who held "fiefs" or possessions directly from the king, which consisted of manors in various parts of the country —sometimes a number of manors pretty close together, but often with big stretches of unoccupied land between them over which the king had full control. Out of these unused districts the king could, and often did make new grants of land.

As years rolled on, the manors became more valuable, and new manors were formed. In the earlier days the manor and the parish meant much the same thing; but in course of time, though the boundaries of the parish did not alter much, the number of manors increased in some parishes from one to two or three, or even more.

In many cases the mode of life on these manors went on unchanged for centuries, the tenants of these different manors going to the original parish church and the parish priest ministering to the people in all the manors in his parish. In other cases daughter churches, or chapels of ease, were built in the newer manors, and provision was made for the support of a priest to minister to them. These have in some instances been erected in the course of time into separate parishes; but many remained as parts of the mother parish, though they might be several miles away from the parish church.

All through the Norman times there was a tendency to make new manors, and this gave rise to so many

G

difficulties that the practice was stopped in the time of King Edward I.

In all parts of England to-day we have parks belonging to big mansions; and our big towns and cities have their parks too; but these are usually recreation-grounds for the people, and most of them are quite modern, with bandstands and sports' grounds, clumps of shrubs, flower-beds, and stretches of greensward. A park in Norman and in Early English times was very different in appearance from our parks, whether in town or country. Just as the king had his great forests for hunting wild beasts, so in the later Norman times the great lords were anxious to enclose pieces of waste and forest land for the same purpose.

As we have seen, there were in early times vast tracts of wild, uncultivated, unenclosed land, partly wooded and partly heath land, between the manors, which belonged to the king. The king alone could give leave to make a park. In the reign of King Henry III especially we find many such parks were "empaled". Of course the nobles had to give something to the king for this privilege.

Many of the old parks in England, now celebrated for their fine timber and beautiful scenery, date back to this period; but they were at first much wilder, and the trees then were neither so many nor so fine as they are now. The deer remaining in some of them to-day just serve to remind us of the "wild beasts" with which they were stocked.

The laws for preserving the wild beasts and the game in these parks and forests and chases were very strict, harsh, and severe. Many of these new parks took away from the villeins, who lived in the neighbourhood, certain rights and privileges which their forefathers had had "time out of mind".

Though the land could not be bought and sold out-

Manor House, Thirteenth Century

Built by Robert Burnell, Bishop of Bath, and Chancellor to Edward I at Acton Burnell, Shropshire.

right, manors became divided and subdivided, let and underlet, for various terms of years, and in many curious ways, so that in time the profits, or the income, of a manor, instead of going straight to the lord of the manor, might be going to half a dozen different persons and places. For instance, the half of a manor might be divided amongst several people for, say, twenty years, or for the lives of three or four people; but at the end of the twenty years, or on the death of the last of those persons, it must go back to the lord of the manor, who could keep it in his hands or let it out in other ways to quite a different set of people.

It is not very difficult to understand that the management of an estate of many manors, broken up into many small portions, became very complicated. Records of all these various transactions had to be made in writing and carefully kept, and copied and re-copied time after

time.   People who understood all the "ins and outs" of
the laws relating to the possession of land became very
important and very busy.

There are immense numbers of documents, some of
them dating back to Norman and even earlier times,
still in existence.   The Record Office, in London, has
many thousands of documents connected with the king's
business; the borough towns and cities and the monasteries each had their own records, but most of these
latter records disappeared in the sixteenth century;
every old estate has such documents; and many of the
old manors have still records going back many centuries.
Of course thousands more of these old documents have
been lost, some destroyed purposely, and others through
carelessness and ignorance.   Some have been burnt in
times of danger, when their owner, knowing that there
were documents amongst them which might get him
into trouble and cost him his head, set fire to bundles
of papers and parchments.   Others have been stored
away in dark, damp cellars and forgotten for years and
years, and rats and mice have nibbled them away, or
mildew and damp have caused them to rot.

Those that we have left can still be read, and it is
surprising to find in many cases how well they have
been preserved all through the centuries.   The letters
are very often beautifully formed, and the whole clear
and distinct.   They were written in Norman French and
Latin, the latter being the language in which law business was carried on for many centuries.[1]

[1] Notice a fine specimen, written before the Conquest, given on p. 103, and the
illustration facing p. 88.

CHAPTER XXVIII

Traces of Early Times in the Churches

In most villages the church is the chief old building
in the place, and it is a good thing to be able to tell the
time to which its different parts belong. It will help us
to fix in our minds the different periods, or steps, in the
history of our country.

A little party of holiday-makers were one day strolling
through a country churchyard in which was a very old
church. They were not much interested until one of
the party saw in the wall of the church a slab to "an
honest carpenter", dated 1765. "How very, very old!"
he exclaimed, and called the attention of his companions
to it, and they all wondered and marvelled. Yet in that
same wall were bits of work which belonged to a past
age, not just a hundred or so years back, but a thousand
years back. They had not been trained to read "the
signs of the times".

Never be ashamed to ask questions about an old building. It will be a very strange thing indeed if you cannot find, in every town and village, *somebody* who has
a keen interest in old buildings and who will delight in
pointing them out to you. Nearly every local newspaper
in the country, from time to time, prints odds and ends
connected with the history of the neighbourhood. If
there is anything about an old building that you want
explained, you can easily write a short letter to the editor
of the paper, and there is sure to be someone who will
take the trouble to answer your question, and help you
to understand, and to distinguish between things "that
differ".

Saxon Window,
Wyckham, Berks

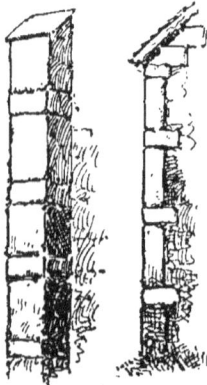

Long and Short Work
(Saxon)

Saxon Doorway,
Barton

Norman
Carving

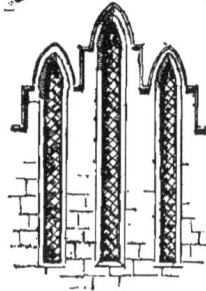

Norman Doorway, Castle Rising,
Norfolk

Lancet
Window

Fourteenth-century Doorway,
Adderbury, Oxford

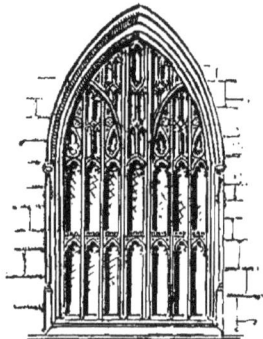

Fifteenth-century Window

Saxon, Norman, and Later Architectural Features

An old parish church has a good deal to tell us about the history of the parish and its people, and if you know something of the history of the place in which you live you will know something *worth knowing* of the history of your country, which will help you to be a good citizen. But this knowledge can only be picked up little by little, and you cannot learn "all about it" in the course of a few days.

There are, as we said in a former chapter, some few churches which have little bits of Saxon work left in their walls and windows. In a great many more we shall see some Norman work, especially in pillars and arches and doorways. That Norman Period takes in the reigns of all the kings from William I to the time of King John, from the middle of the eleventh century to the end of the twelfth, down to the time of Magna Carta.

When we come to the time of Magna Carta we are in the thirteenth century, when pointed arches came into use. Through the reigns of King Henry III and King Edward I a great deal of building in that style went on. In almost every parish some alteration was made in the church in that century; and probably in the chancel there are one or two old windows which will be pointed out to you as having been first put in during that century.[1]

You may perhaps find a very old battered figure of a man in chain armour, the sort of armour in which King Edward I went fighting in the Third Crusade, in Wales, and in Scotland; in which Simon de Montfort and Wallace and the Bruce fought. Some of these effigies have the legs crossed—some at the ankles, some at the knees, and some at the thighs. It used to be said that these represented crusaders; but nobody seems really to know what was the meaning of the cross-legged effigies.

[1] In the "Lancet Windows", shown in the illustration on p. 94, you have a specimen of that thirteenth-century or Early-English style.

Then there are some flat stones, lying in the pavement, with inscriptions running round the edge in strange worn letters, with perhaps an ornamental cross also cut the whole length of the stones. These are the cover-stones of the graves where some great baron or landowner was buried, and they belong to the thirteenth century, and some are even of earlier date. They are called incised slabs.

In this same century another kind of cover-stone for a grave came into use, especially in the southern and eastern parts of England. Metal was fixed in the incised slabs, and the portrait of the knight and his lady, the merchant or the lawyer, the bishop or priest, was engraved on the metal, showing the person in the kind of dress worn during life. It is said that there are about four thousand of these brasses still left in England. Some of them have been sadly damaged and worn. They do not all belong to the thirteenth century, as this kind of memorial of the dead was used during several centuries — in fact, well on into Queen Elizabeth's reign, at the end of the sixteenth century. The oldest brass in England, showing a man in armour, is in Surrey, in Stoke D'Abernon church. Brasses are very valuable, as they show us the kinds of armour and dress worn in particular centuries.

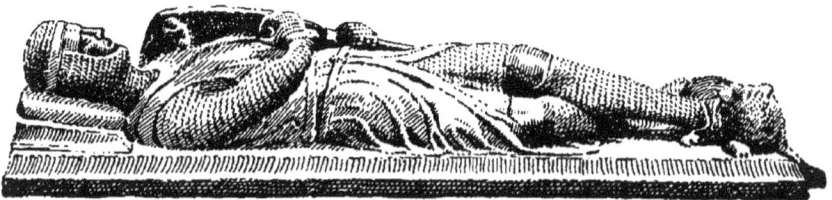

Effigy with Crossed Legs in the Temple Church, London

The feet are placed upon a lion, indicating, it is said, that the knight took part in the Crusades and was killed in action.

CHAPTER XXIX

Traces of Early Times in the Churches (*Cont.*)

The fourteenth century is covered by the reigns of King Edward II, King Edward III, and King Richard II. The architecture became much more ornamental, and there is a good deal of fine stone-carving.[1] Many beautiful window-heads and doorways belong to this period. A good many aisles were added to the old naves; many of the old Norman towers were rebuilt and crowned with graceful spires; but the work is not all equally good.

It will be noticed that the most beautiful spires are very frequently met with in districts that are flat and destitute of the natural beauty which mountains and hills, valleys and woodlands, give to a landscape; and it looks as if the people in different parishes had tried to outdo their neighbours in erecting graceful spires on their church towers.

There are a great many tombs in the churches in various parts of the country, and much money was spent upon them in this and in the next century. They are raised some two or three feet from the ground; the sides are divided into panels and ornamented with rich carvings and shields of arms, brilliantly coloured and gilded. On the top of the tombs are to be seen effigies carved in stone of the man and his wife, lying on their backs, with hands clasped. The men are usually in armour, and their wives in the dress of the time, with strange-looking head-dresses. Many of the effigies are much defaced and battered, but there are others of them well

[1] See " Fourteenth-century Doorway ", on p. 94, for a specimen of this style.

preserved still. It was in the latter part of the fourteenth century that great attention began to be paid to shields of arms, and heraldry became an important science.

But in the middle of the fourteenth century, during the reign of King Edward III, there came a time of great distress. There were the long years of war with France, years of famine and the Black Death. That meant a period of great distress for the country; all classes suffered, and there was much discontent and disorder. These bad times left their marks upon the buildings, especially upon the churches. In some churches work can be pointed out to you which was begun before the time of the Black Death on a grand scale, but finished off in a much plainer manner— apparently years after it was begun. The work had been started, but bad times stopped it, and it had to wait. Those who had begun it never saw it finished, for the pestilence carried them away; and, long afterwards, those who did finish it were not well enough off to carry out the design as it was at first intended.

Still, all through these centuries much was spent on the churches, not only by the great nobles, not only in monastery buildings and the cathedral churches, but on the ordinary town and village churches as well.

The wealthy wool-merchants, especially in the fourteenth century, spent much on the building and decoration of churches. Some of the finest churches in the eastern and western counties of England owe much to them. Then, too, it was quite a common thing for the various trade guilds in a town to have a little chapel, or an aisle, or an altar in the parish church, which the guild undertook to keep up. One guild tried to outdo the others in this matter. All the craftsmen of those days belonged to a trade guild of some sort, and much good artistic work was done, which found a place in the churches.

People took a keen interest in their churches, and we find them leaving money towards their upkeep, towards making a statue, or doing some carving, or even keeping a light burning. Whatever may have been their reasons for so doing, the fact that they did so is very clear.

They used their churches in ways that may seem strange to us; but they looked upon them as their own, and were evidently in many cases proud of them. Each parish annually chose its churchwardens, who had charge of the buildings and the furniture, and these were responsible to the bishop, as well as to the people of the parish. Every now and then the bishop visited the parish, or sent someone to do so in his name. Enquiry was made as to how the priest and the people carried out their duties towards each other. Complaints were heard, and attempts made to set matters right. Some of the reports which were made on such occasions have come down to us, and show often much disorder, and at times much that was evil. But

Spire of Norwich Cathedral
Fourteenth Century

we must not forget that good was also being done then, which was not talked much about.

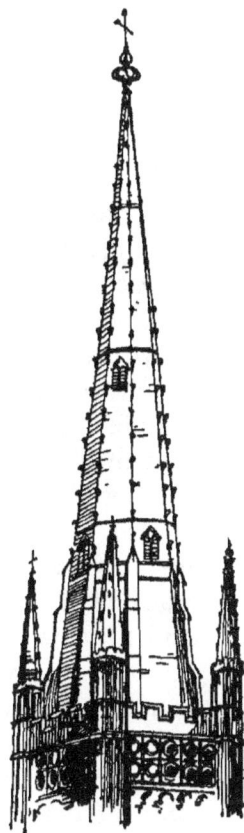

> "The evil that men do lives after them,
> The good is oft interred with their bones."

CHAPTER XXX

Clerks

Changes took place much more slowly in the Middle Ages than they do now. First of all, the population was very much smaller, and hundreds and hundreds of acres now covered by big manufacturing towns were then unoccupied land.

At the time of the Norman Conquest the whole population of England only numbered about two million people; and in the time of King Henry VII it was only four millions; so that in the course of four hundred years the population had only doubled itself.

The people were not crowded into the towns. For instance, in the time of King Edward III, Colchester was one of the large towns, yet it had only three hundred and fifty houses, in which three thousand people lived, all told. There were only nine larger towns in the country at that time.

The bulk of the people were living in the villages, in the various manors, not in the towns. Many things prevented the population from growing very rapidly—disease, famine, and war kept it down. Death was the punishment for a very large number of offences, so that it is not to be wondered at that the population did not increase very fast.

The population was divided into two distinct classes—those who were clergy, or clerks, and those who were not. By "clergy" we understand, in these days, "ministers of religion"; but the word had a very different meaning in the Middle Ages.

In early Saxon times religion and learning were very closely related. Colleges and monasteries were centres of learning, and bishops, abbots, priests, and monks took

A Scriptorium with clerk writing

After a miniature in a manuscript in the Bibliothèque Nationale

the lead in matters in which a knowledge of reading and writing was required. Folk who had a leaning towards learning naturally became connected with colleges or monasteries. They began as scholars, and then were admitted, or ordained, to one of the lower orders of the ministry—often when they were still only boys.

There are many thousands of boys to-day who are choir-boys. In early times those admitted to such an office as that had to be ordained, or set apart for the purpose, by the bishop. That ordaining made them clerks or clergy; and they were then under the authority of the bishop or his officers. If they did wrong, they were tried and punished in the bishop's court.

In the course of years there grew up, side by side, two different set of courts of justice, the Church Courts and the King's Courts, which were each guided by different laws. The laws which ruled the Church Courts were much more merciful than those which ruled the civil or King's Courts. Death was the punishment for almost every offence tried in the King's Courts and in the Manor Courts; but in the Church Courts the punishments were much less severe, and the culprit had a much better chance of "turning over a new leaf".

If a man was brought before the King's Court charged with a crime, he could call for a book. If he could read a few sentences, that was taken to show that he was a clerk, and he could claim to be tried by the Church Court. That is, he could claim "benefit of clergy".

You can readily see that such a state of things, however good it may have been at the first, was dreadfully abused in the course of time. What at first had been merciful and just became in time mischievous and dangerous. The great struggle between King Henry II and Archbishop Thomas à Becket had to do with the power of these two sets of courts, the King's Courts and the Church Courts—it had to do with government, *not* with religion and religious matters.

Clerks, or the clergy, were drawn from all classes of society, from the royal family down to the serfs on the manors. In fact, before the time of the Black Death, the only way in which a serf could become a freeman was by buying his freedom or by becoming a clerk. A serf who wanted his son to rise to a better position than his own would try to get him made a clerk; for the moment he became a clerk he was a free man. But to attain his purpose the serf must first have the permission of his master or overlord. All overlords were not tyrants by any means. The serf might do his master a good turn—save his life, for instance—and in return his master would set him free, or allow his son to be taught by the

priest and ordained; or he might let him join a college
or monastery.

Many and many a priest, clerk, or monk rose from
being a serf or a villein in this way; so many, in fact,
that a writer in the twelfth century complains that villeins
were attempting "to educate their ignoble offspring".
Later still, Piers Plowman complains that "bondsmen's
bairns could be made bishops".

There was a very sharp line of division between clerks
and those who were not clerks, and the privileges which
clerks had, led to much squabbling and many disorders.

Kings and nobles employed clerks on their business,
for the simple reason that they were able men, and had
some "book learning", and so, in that way, were better
educated than most of those who were not clerks. From
the clerks, too, were drawn the men whom we now call
lawyers. We have seen that there was a vast deal of
writing to be done in those days in connection with the
towns and the manors. Among these clerks were good
men and bad men: some who loved learning for its own
sake; some who found that it paid better than anything
else; and others who misused their privileges, did much
evil, and brought the name of "clerk" into sad disgrace.

*Writing before the Norman Conquest. From a charter of Cnut (1018)
now in the British Museum*

CHAPTER XXXI

Fairs

The word "Fair" calls up to our minds all sorts of wonderful sights and sounds—the stalls with their wonderful "fairings" and "goodies"; the shows and the shooting-galleries; the "flying horses", the "conjurors", the performing dogs, and Punch and Judy; the wonderful caravans and coco-nuts; the musical instruments of all sorts, from the mouth-organ and "squeaker" to the steam-organ of the roundabout.

Many such fairs are still held in every county and they connect the present day very closely with the life of bygone days. It is "all the fun of the fair" which draws people to them mostly nowadays, but in some of them there is still important business done; people are attracted to them for trade as well as for pleasure.

Some of these fairs are held in big towns, such as Lincoln and Carlisle. At Barnet a great horse fair is held every year in September. But some big fairs are held away from any large town, such as the big sheep fair at Weyhill, in Hampshire. At Stourbridge, in Cambridgeshire, a fair is still held; it is quite an ordinary one now, but in the Middle Ages it was one of the most important fairs, not only in England, but in Europe —a great gathering, where East and West met to do business with each other.

In some places the business part of the fair has quite died out, and a few stalls, a roundabout, a shooting-gallery, and swings are all that can be seen on a fairday.

The word "fair" comes from an old word which means a "feast" or festival. There are many villages which still have their annual village feast, more important to the

CASTLE AND BUTTER MARKET, DUNSTER, SOMERSETSHIRE

[See page 129]

village than Christmas or a "Bank Holiday". Houses are turned out and cleaned from top to bottom; everything must be made fit to be seen "for the feast". It is a great meeting-time for families, and the boys and girls who have gone away to work in some big town try to get back for a few hours to their native village, to "the old house at home".

In the beginning the village feast was connected with the parish church—it was the festival of the saint after whom the church was named. That day was a holiday, and all the people went to church as a matter of course. The church was the gathering-place, and, in the porch and the churchyard, and on the village green, friends, neighbours, and relatives met and had a time of rejoicing.

So many people coming together attracted pedlars and hawkers, who spread out their goods on the green, in the churchyard, and in the church porch itself. People who met but seldom used the chance of doing a little business with each other. Little by little, then, the "feast" became a "fair", and in many cases was a very important business and trading meeting.

Now it did not suit the ideas of people in those days that outsiders should come into their village and buy and sell as they chose. You know how the boys living in one street even nowadays object to the boys from another street coming to play in their street—"You go and play in your own street". So in very early times the lord of the manor began to regulate these things. Outsiders who brought their goods for sale had to pay a "due" or "toll" to the lord of the manor to be allowed to trade; and the right of receiving tolls for fairs became one of an overlord's privileges.

The people in the towns, who were more interested in trade than the people in the villages, saw how very important and profitable a fair was—that it was something "with money in it"—and the towns were very anxious to get the right to hold one or more annual fairs. But the overlord, the king, had a voice in the matter, because each stall set up, and each bale of goods, brought in " by right " an income.

The king had the right to grant, almost to whom he pleased, the privilege of holding a fair; and the privilege was much sought after. Towns, as we saw in a former chapter, got charters from the king, which very often gave to them this right. But it was quite a common thing for the king to make a grant of an annual fair to a religious house which he wanted to benefit without much cost to himself, and the profits of the fair went to support the house. The king's nobles did the same kind of thing in their own domains.

All the shops in the place where the fair was held had to be shut while the fair was on, and nothing could be bought or sold except in the fair. The tradesmen of the place had to pay their tolls to the person or public body to whom the fair had been granted, just as the strangers coming into the town did.

Fairs lasted in some cases for only one day; in others for two, three, or more days, and sometimes as long as a fortnight, during which time, whether the inhabitants liked it or not, all trade had to be carried on only in the fair. That was one of the things which caused jealousy between the trading class and the religious houses, and often led to much ill-feeling and disorder.

Then, too, the king could grant to any person the right to go to any fair in the country without paying toll and duty. Of course those persons to whom the king granted this right had to pay him very heavily for this privilege, but you can see that it was quite worth their while. Foreign merchants and Jews[1] often had such privileges granted to them, and that partly accounts

[1] The Jews were expelled from England A.D. 1290.

for the great dislike there was to these classes of people.

Many of the religious houses had entered into trade too, and very often the same privilege of putting their goods on the market was granted to them. Members of a religious house could often travel from place to place without having to pay any of the tolls and duties which other folk had to pay. That might be quite right and reasonable when they were on some religious duty or errand of mercy, but when it was connected with buying and selling the goods produced or manufactured on the monastery lands it was "rather hard", as we should say, on the traders. The grievance grew up gradually, but it caused very often a bitter feeling between the towns and the religious houses in them, which over and over again led to riots and bloodshed.

Morris Dancers, Fourteenth Century

From an illuminated manuscript in the Bodleian Library, Oxford.

CHAPTER XXXII

Markets

One of the pleasantest sights, to a Londoner at any rate, is the market-place of an old-fashioned country town on a market-day. In many such towns the weekly market is held, in the open air, in the same place where it has been held for centuries. Probably none of the houses round the market-square is as old as the market, but the buildings, altered and rebuilt as they have been, take us back several centuries, and speak of days long gone by.

A good many towns have built covered markets. Some of them are near the old market-place, but in other cases the market is now held in quite another part of the town. Cattle-markets, which used to be held in the open street in a busy thoroughfare, are now often held in places more suitable for that purpose some distance away from their old quarters.

Corn-markets are held in most market-towns, frequently on the same day as the general market, and many towns now boast a corn-exchange. Then, too, in some places there are markets held in connection with the chief trade of the neighbourhood.

The market-house is often a curious building. You may almost speak of it as "a big room on legs". There is a large room standing on stone or wooden arches. The open space underneath serves to shelter some of the market-stalls, and a staircase leads up from the street to the room above, where the town council holds its meetings. On the roof of this building is a turret containing a clock, and perhaps a fire-bell and a market-bell. There is such a quaint old market-house still standing at Amersham, in Buckinghamshire, but so many of these old buildings have been pulled down to make way for larger structures, in which the town can carry on its business, and where the various officers can have their offices, that the town hall is mostly now a smart modern building.

Market Cross and Portion of Shelter, Winchester

The stalls set up on the market-day are of the same simple kind as those which have been used for centuries. It is curious to notice how the different trades keep to different parts of the market-place—butchers in one place, greengrocers in another, and fishmongers in another. Just as the trades had their special quarters in the town, so they had in the market. Things have altogether changed as far as the shops are concerned, but the setting out of the market is almost exactly the same to-day as it was five hundred years ago.

The market cross still remains in some towns, but the cross itself has in many cases disappeared long ago. In some places the steps and the lower part of the cross still remain, but there is a kind of open shed built round it to form a shelter. Some of these shelters are very ornamental, like those at Chichester and Winchester.[1] It is not an uncommon thing for such a cross as that to be called the Butter Cross,[2] from the fact that around the cross was held the butter-market. Some of these shelters are quaint rather than beautiful, and cover the town pump, which is now carefully locked up. In some places a drinking-fountain stands where once the cross stood. At the cross a good deal of business was done. The mayor or his officers would read out public notices there on the market-day, that everybody might hear. Not far from the cross was the cage, where folk who had been "taken up" were set for a time. The stocks, the pillory, and the whipping-post, in the seventeenth century, were usually here in the market-place, not far from the cross.

There is much to see in a market-place on a market-day. If the market-day is Saturday, you will find the place thronged with people, especially at night; and even quite small towns are then so crowded that you wonder where the people come from.

Fairs, in the Middle Ages, provided for much of the wholesale trade of the country, and markets for the retail trade. The two were very much alike, and the rights

---

[1] This was built in the fifteenth century; but of course it has been restored since then. At the end of the eighteenth century the authorities of the city actually sold it to a gentleman who proposed to place it in his own pleasure-ground; but the people of the city drove away the workmen who were sent to remove it, and so it had to remain in its ancient place.

[2] Such a Butter Cross is seen in the view of Dunster, facing p. 105.

*Market Scene in the Middle Ages.   The market cross is taken from an old
print of the market cross at Malmesbury
(Note the Pillory, the Whipping-post, and the Stocks.)*

to hold an annual fair and a weekly market mostly went
together.

Some places had, and still have, more than one market
a week.   In many places the market has quite died out
now, but in the early days one of the first steps of a
"tun" towards becoming a "town" was to obtain the
right to hold a market.   There are many of our modern

towns which have grown up in manufacturing districts, near great railway centres, or near docks and railway stations, which have no market. Nearly all of our old towns have, or at one time *had*, the right of holding markets.

Nobody can set up a stall in a market as he pleases. On the market-day you will see the beadle going about from stall to stall taking the toll from each stall-holder. In many cases he wears an old-fashioned dress trimmed with gold lace. He reminds us of the time when no one except a freeman of the town could trade freely. The stall-holders were "foreigners", and had to pay to the town a toll for permission to sell in the town. In our day you can go and settle in any town you please, and open a shop just as you like, but you cannot so easily take a stall and sell in the market: you must pay the market toll even now. Such tolls go towards the expenses of the town.

In the market the town and the country meet. In these days, when the produce of the country can be quickly sent into the heart of the largest town, the country provision-markets are not of as much importance as they once were, but they are very useful and very popular still.

There are many places where the market beadle rings a hand-bell, or a bell in the clock-tower, to give notice of the opening and closing of the market. In former days, if a man dared to sell anything before the bell was rung in the morning, or after it had rung in the evening, he was very severely punished. Even now, goods may not be sold in the market before or after the regular market hours.

There were proper town officers appointed by the mayor and corporation to look after the markets, and to see that goods were sold at the proper market price, and that there was no cheating in weight and measure, and in the quality of the goods sold.

CHAPTER XXXIII

Schools

The earliest schools in England were held in the monasteries, and were intended for boys and young men who were to be trained as priests, missionaries, or monks. There were famous schools at Canterbury, York, and Jarrow in the seventh and eighth centuries. In King Alfred's time, at the end of the ninth century, great attention was paid to the teaching of both boys and girls. Later still, in the tenth century, we find the teaching of the young attracting great attention.

Latin was taught in these schools, and many of the scholars became famous students and deep thinkers. In the course of time others, besides those intending to become monks and priests, were also taught, and became clerks and found various employments, as we have seen, in civil business.

Gradually other schools sprang up, outside the monasteries and cathedrals, which were not meant for monks or priests, though they were at first connected with monasteries, colleges, and cathedrals. For instance, in Norman times, not very long after the Conquest, there were grammar-schools at Derby, St. Alban's, and Bury St. Edmund's.

When we think of these schools we must not picture to ourselves great buildings to hold two or three hundred boys, such as we see now; nor must we suppose that there was a great rush of pupils to them. Boys did not go to school from nine till twelve, and from two till four, with plenty of time for cricket, football, and sports of all descriptions. School work was very hard, and was regarded as a serious business. There was a great deal of learning by heart to be done. You see, books were few and costly, and a man's best reference library was his own well-stored memory. No doubt this hard work helped to train the memory, and was good discipline for the scholar.

In the monasteries and colleges, where boys were trained to sing in the choir, they had to learn their services by heart; for books were not provided for them—a book was much too valuable in days when they were all written by hand, and when printing first came into use they were still far too costly for ordinary monks and choir-boys to have one apiece, or even enough for several to "look over". In the ordinary services there were long psalms and passages of Scripture attached to them which differed for every day, and the boys had to know these perfectly in Latin. For hours and hours every day the little fellows were drilled in the services till they were word-perfect. There were something like seven services to be learned for each of the three hundred and sixty-five days of the year.

We talk of Latin nowadays as a dead language, but it was anything but a dead language in the Middle Ages. School was held all day long from quite early in the morning; and during school-hours woe betide the lads if they talked in any other language but Latin.

Choir-boys had to be taught in the song-school as well, how to sing their services, and the music was just as difficult as the words and had also to be learned by heart.

In the parish churches the priest and the parish clerk had boys whom they trained to help in the services. The services were much simpler and shorter than those in the monasteries; but they were in Latin, and had to be known by heart.

In the grammar and other schools the boys were drilled in the works of old Latin scholars in much the

A School, Fourteenth Century

From an illuminated manuscript in the Bodleian Library, Oxford.

same way, and in some cases in Greek authors as well, with a certain amount of arithmetic and science.

There were no long weeks of holidays to look forward to at Christmas, Easter, Whitsuntide, and in the summer; but during the year there were many holy days kept, which were holidays, on which neither school-boys nor villeins did their ordinary work. Thus, no doubt, schoolboys managed to get a fair amount of play, and found time for getting into mischief.

For instance, at St. Alban's we read that in the year 1310 the boys were forbidden to wander or run about the streets and roads without reasonable cause. If a lad did so, he was to be sought for and punished by the master "in the accustomed way"; and every boy knows what that was. Then, too, the scholars must not bear arms, either in school or out of school. That was to prevent them from fighting with the townspeople. It is very curious to notice that even nowadays there is often no love lost between "grammar boys" and "town boys"; they can get up a quarrel almost as easily in the twentieth century as they did in the thirteenth. It shows itself whenever there happens to be a heavy fall of snow, and sometimes tempers get "lost, or mislaid".

Boys took part in acting the earliest plays that were represented in England. At first the plays dealt with religious subjects, and were called "Mysteries" and "Miracles"; and these plays and shows became very popular in England. Geoffrey de Gorham, in early Norman days, taught a school at Dunstable, and wrote one of these plays called St. Catherine. He borrowed vestments from St. Alban's Abbey, in which to dress some of his characters; but on the following night his house somehow caught fire, and his books and the borrowed vestments were destroyed in the flames.

In the cloisters of some of our old cathedral churches and colleges, such as Gloucester and Westminster, on some of the old stone benches, there are holes and scratches still to be seen where schoolboys of long ago played games with marbles and stones.

By the thirteenth century there seem to have been schools in all the chief towns. Though they may not have held very many scholars, they were not intended for the sons of well-to-do people only; they were for poor scholars as well. Thus, at St. Alban's, provision was made for sixteen poor scholars, and the same kind of provision was quite common. There was some chance, even in those days, for a lad with "brains" to get on in the world. In fact, we know that in those Middle Ages a good many men rose "from the ranks" to hold high office in the state. There was, for instance, Thomas à Becket. He was born in London, and not ashamed to be known as Thomas of London. Then there was Thomas Scot, who rose to be Archbishop of York and Chancellor of England in the fifteenth century, who was known as Thomas of Rotherham, after the place where he was born. William of Wykeham, that great founder of schools, is still known by the name of the little out-of-the-way Hampshire village where he was born—Wyke-ham. Winchester College, the first of our public schools, was founded by him. His real surname was Longe, and the motto he chose—"Manners Makyth Man"—is worth putting up in every school in the land. We need to live up to that motto as much in these days as ever.

But there were dunces in those days too, who made little or no use of their opportunities, and others who turned them to bad purposes, even as there are in this twentieth century.

Part of Winchester College, built in 1692

CHAPTER XXXIV

Universities

Now, just as the tide flows and ebbs, so in England did interest in learning rise and fall during the Middle Ages. Schools of all kinds had their good times and their bad times. Sometimes we find the thirst for learning being shown in one direction; then it almost died away for a time, revived again, and took another direction.

At first we see it going in the direction of making monks and priests and missionaries; then in that of making able men who could take part in the civil business of the manor, the town, and the country; and then, in the thirteenth century, it began again to take a turn towards learning for learning's sake.

As we get near to the thirteenth century, we find the beginnings of our English universities. A university was a corporation or body of learned men who bound themselves together to teach, and who got the sole right of appointing teachers in their districts. A man could only have leave to teach after his knowledge and ability had been well tried by them; and when that leave was given he was said to take his degree.

The opportunity of getting wider knowledge and higher teaching attracted scholars, lads and young men who had had their early teaching in the small colleges and grammar-schools. They were encouraged and in many ways helped to go to the university. Gifts were left to their old schools to help the likely boys to go to the university; many of the monasteries and colleges sent their pupils there, and it was looked upon as a pious work and a work of mercy to help poor scholars in this way.

Scholars flocked in hundreds to various universities, and we find Oxford and Cambridge rising as university towns. We cannot say exactly when this began, but we read that in King John's reign, in the year 1209, there was a great "town and gown" riot at Oxford. Three of the gownsmen were hanged as a punishment; so about three thousand of the rest left Oxford and went to

Gloucester Hall, now Worcester College, Oxford, founded 1283

From a drawing made in 1673, when a considerable portion of the thirteenth-century building still remained little altered.

other universities, and Oxford was deserted for a time. These facts show that by the beginning of the thirteenth century, just when the Early English style of architecture was coming into fashion, universities, with their "higher education", were very important institutions.

At first it seems that the scholars at the university lived in the town, where they chose or where they could, attending the various lecture-halls. Then various people seem to have hit upon the plan of setting up houses in the town, and letting the rooms to the scholars, so that a number of them might live together. Thus they were divided up into different sets. These houses were called hostels, and we find them at Cambridge in the beginning of the thirteenth century.

Early, too, in this same century a new religious order found its way to England—the Friars. The Dominican Friars were a very learned teaching order, and when they settled at Oxford they greatly strengthened the work of the university and kept it alive and active.

A Surrey man, Walter de Merton, Chancellor and Bishop of Rochester, was the inventor or founder of colleges at the universities such as we know them to-day. In the hostels the scholars did pretty much as they pleased, chose their own officers, and made their own rules. There was much disorder after a while; many quarrels and fights took place between one hostel and another, as well as with the townsfolk. Merton spent twelve years in thinking out his plan, and at last, in the year 1264, he founded or established the first of the Oxford Colleges.

The old monasteries and colleges in the early times had been founded to keep up a continual round of worship, work, and learning; the special work of these new colleges was to promote learning and fellowship. In many ways they were like the older convents; but the work of education was the chief object of these new foundations, and we find teachers and taught, governors and pupils, living under the same roof, under rule and order.

Merton's idea was soon afterwards followed at Cambridge, where Peterhouse was opened in the year 1284. During this century, too, we find a rival university springing up at Stamford; in fact in the year 1333 a number of masters and scholars left Oxford for Stamford; but, owing to the opposition of Oxford and Cam-

CLOISTER QUADRANGLE, MAGDALEN COLLEGE, OXFORD

.

bridge, it was gradually snuffed out, though there are still standing some interesting buildings which were connected with it. College after college, at both Oxford and Cambridge, has been founded since then; each one has its own special laws and government, which have been altered from time to time. For many centuries now Oxford and Cambridge have been cities of colleges, and these "ancient seats of learning" are quite unlike any other places in the country.

Many old customs are kept up still at Oxford and Cambridge; the scholars and officials of the colleges and universities go about in their gowns, as they have done for centuries, and each university has still rights and privileges in the government of the town which have naturally come to it in the course of time. The town and the townsfolk have their special interests and government; so that there are two authorities, side by side, responsible for law and order. The gown and the town depend upon each other; and in days gone by they have, times without number, misunderstood each other, and quarrelled, and fought.

In the reign of King Edward III Oxford was the most famous seat of learning in Europe. Many of its students were foreigners, but, as everyone could talk Latin as well as he could his native language, they had no real difficulty in making themselves understood.

Within the last hundred years, in order to meet modern requirements, universities have been founded at Durham, London, Liverpool, Birmingham, Manchester, Leeds, Sheffield, and Bristol.

Gownsman of Fifteenth Century. From an old print of Chaucer's Clerk of Oxenford

CHAPTER XXXV

Changes Brought About by the Black Death

In the middle of the fourteenth century, in the reign of King Edward III, came the Black Death. It carried off half the population of the country at least, and all classes of society felt its effects.

We have said that in some of the old parish churches you can see, by some of the work done just after this time, that the builders were very much poorer than they had been, and had to finish off in a very plain fashion work begun on a grand scale. You must remember, too, that there were several different kinds of landowners or overlords—the king, the great lords, bishops, colleges, and monasteries. The manors, of which these estates were made up, in the course of centuries were divided and subdivided in many ways as the land became more valuable. Many people might thus have an interest in one manor which a couple of hundred years before had been in the hands of one person only. That made law business very complicated when these little parcels of land changed hands.

Though manors could not be bought and sold outright, little by little money was paid to have bits of manors and the various rights in manors let out, or leased, for a term of years. This was especially the case with property in towns, and with lands belonging to corporations, like colleges and monasteries, which were often scattered about in various parts of the country.

On the manors in the country districts the same thing

was going on, though perhaps more slowly than in the towns. It became much more convenient for the villeins and cottiers, and other tenants of a manor, to pay a rent to the lord instead of actually working on the lord's land. At first this rent was paid in the produce of the land—a few hens or eggs, a calf or a lamb, or so much corn, till by and by we find actual payments in money as rent.

Then, too, a class of labourers had gradually sprung up on the manors. As the tenants and villeins began to pay to the lord a quit-rent, instead of working so many days a week on the land, the lord of the manor had to employ persons to do the work on his home-farm. These would naturally be the cottiers and serfs on the manor—the "landless men"—who thus became what we know as labourers.

All these had to be accounted for in the manor court, which was held regularly every few weeks. If a labourer was missing he was sought for, and brought back to the manor, which he might not leave without his lord's permission. It is quite true that if he could only remain unclaimed in some borough town for a year and a day he was no longer bound to the lord of his native manor; but the towns did not encourage strangers, as we have seen. If, however, labour happened to be wanted in the town, no doubt his being there would be "winked at" and no notice would be taken of his "harbouring" there; and in this way numbers managed to get their freedom.

But it was not an easy matter for a labourer to get away from his native manor. After the Black Death, labour became very scarce, for on some of the manors almost every tenant and labourer died. All over the country land-workers were wanted badly; and tenants and landlords, when they were so hard pushed, were glad to employ almost any man who appeared, and they

did not trouble to ask whose " man he was " or whence
he came.

The wages of the labourers, of course, went up; but
before very long the landlords saw that that would not
do; it made their farming so much more expensive, and
so their incomes tended to grow less and less.   Law
after law was passed to get the labourers back to
their native manors, and to keep down the price of
labour.

All classes of overlords, and especially the colleges
and monasteries, had much difficulty in working their
lands, and so the custom of letting them out in farms
increased a good deal after the Black Death.

At first the owners let out these farms with a certain
amount of stock on them.   They were let for so many
years, or for so many lives.   At the end of the time the
farm had to be given up and the stock replaced as it had
been at the first.   The land belonging to the farm was
mixed up with the land of other tenants in the manor,
in the big unenclosed fields, and had to be farmed still
according to the old customs of the manor.   Some of
the very oldest
farms existing to
this day began in
this kind of way,
and there are
possibly a few
of the very oldest
farmhouses which
were first built
early in the fif-
teenth century.

*Labourers felling a Tree, Fourteenth Century.   From
a manuscript in the British Museum*

CHAPTER XXXVI

Wool

The two great industries of England in the Middle Ages were agriculture and wool-raising, The wool was the finest grown in Europe, and attracted hither merchants from the Continent. They travelled through England—in the Cotswold and Hampshire districts, for instance—and bought wool largely. But in pretty early days England began to manufacture cloth of various kinds; and that, too, became an important article of export. This manufacture was especially strong in the eastern and western parts of the country.

Weavers from Flanders were encouraged to settle in various parts of England, by several of the Norman kings, soon after the Conquest. This was the case in Gloucestershire, for example; but the manufacture declined in the reigns of King John and King Henry III. In the reign of King Edward III it was again introduced.

As the country began to recover from the effects of the Black Death, the cloth trade became a very flourishing industry, and English wool-merchants became a very wealthy and powerful body. These have left their mark on the churches of the land pretty plainly. At the end of the fourteenth century, and in the fifteenth, some of the finest Decorated and Perpendicular work was done, and a large number of churches, especially in Suffolk, Gloucestershire, and Somersetshire, have magnificent towers, which were built at this period. It is pretty safe to say that where to-day you find a little village with a big church—very much larger than the place now needs—with a good deal of work belonging to the Decorated and early Perpendicular periods, that those places were once engaged in some branch or other of the wool and cloth trades.

Many of the fine brasses of which we spoke in a former chapter cover the graves of merchants "of the staple", as these great wool and cloth traders were called. Then, too, some of the very finest timbered houses, with their richly carved fronts, as in Chester and Shrewsbury, were built at this same time.

We have spoken before of the trade guilds. These, too, after the Black Death period, increased in power and wealth. Each guild looked well after the interests of its own craft. It regulated the number of apprentices which a craftsman might have, the hours of work, the rate of pay; it made provision for helping its members in sickness and need; and it saw to burying them decently when they died. Guilds took a lively interest in their parish churches, helped sometimes in forming new schools, hospitals, and alms-houses, and had regular times for meeting together for business and for feasting. They were good to their members, but very hard on those who were not of their number.

From the members of these trade guilds in a town the town guild, or corporation, was formed to rule the town according to its ancient customs and charters, and to obtain for the town as many new rights and privileges as possible. There is much in the corporation of a great city like London, with its many companies, or guilds, which is connected with city life and work of the Middle Ages.

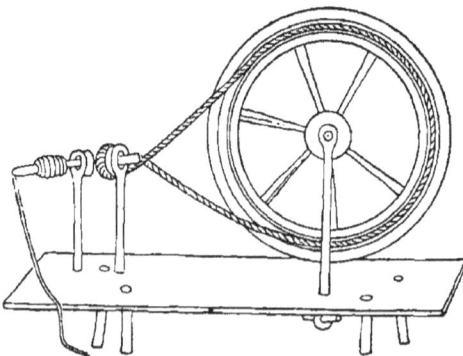

Spinning Wheel, Fourteenth Century

CHAPTER XXXVII

The Poor

From early Christian times in England to relieve the poor was looked upon as a Christian duty, and every church and religious house took its part in the work as a matter of course. You will remember that in early days there was not much moving about of people from one manor to another, so that it was not at first difficult to know the sick and the needy in each place, whether in town or country. Many religious houses or hospitals were founded for the purposes of relief. They were not on a large scale, but there were a good many of them. In the fourteenth century pilgrimages were very popular, and many pilgrims were always to be found on the road.

We must remember that there was another side to a pilgrimage besides the religious one. A pilgrimage was one way of travelling and seeing the world. Indeed it was almost the only means by which a poor man could travel and have change of scene. Permission was given for that purpose because it was regarded as a religious act. It is not at all surprising that folk who wanted to see the world often took advantage of a pilgrimage from no very religious motive. Pilgrims could always find food and lodging at a religious house on their way, and there were scores of places in England to which pilgrimages might be made, to say nothing of a journey to the Holy Land, or to the shrine of St. James of Compostello, which were two grand pilgrimages.

In time pilgrimages became somewhat of a nuisance, for many of the people taking part in them were anything but pious; and, towards the end of the fourteenth century, strict measures were taken to prevent beggars and servants from wandering from one hundred to another on pretence of going on a pilgrimage. Each had to have a letter, properly signed by an officer of the hundred, giving him leave.

But beggars and wanderers increased. We find some towns, in Tudor times, taking steps to put down beggars. In the early part of the sixteenth century vagabonds found in London were to be "tayled[1] at a cart's tayle", and collections were made for the poor weekly, and distributed at the church door. In the year 1536 there were fifteen hospitals and four lazar-houses in the city of London. At the dissolution of the religious houses all these were seized, but the city managed to save St. Mary Spital, St. Thomas's Hospital, and St. Bartholomew's Hospital. The city found that it could not get enough money to keep even one of these going, so a tax was levied for the purpose. Bishop Ridley and others tried to draw up a scheme for finding work for the poor, teaching them to make caps, feather-bed ticks, nails, and ironwork.

Other towns tried the same plan, and the king and Parliament issued many orders about the treatment of the poor and vagabonds. But it was much easier to issue these orders than to carry them out, and the beggars increased in numbers and in impudence in spite of all. In 1547 it was ordained that a sturdy beggar might be made a slave for two years, and, if he ran away, then he was to remain a slave for life. The sons of vagabonds were to be apprenticed till they were twenty-four years old, and their daughters till they were twenty years of age, and, if they rebelled, they were sent to slavery. The idea was to train them to work.

In all this the difficulty was, how to find the money to carry out these schemes. The king had swept away all the goods and gifts which had been made to monas-

---

[1] That is, whipped at a cart's tail.

teries, churches, and hospitals; the free-will offerings of many generations had gone into the pockets of the king; the institutions which had been founded to help the poor had become the private property of the king's favourites. It was not likely that people would be very keen to offer their money for the relief of the poor, and though urged to give what they could, they were very backward in doing so. Later on, in Queen Elizabeth's reign, the dwellers in each parish were urged to find work for the labourers in their parish; but the beggars still wandered and the poor still abounded.

In the year 1571 some very severe laws were made concerning vagabonds. A man who was convicted a third time of being a vagabond was to be punished with death. Habitations were to be found for all the poor belonging to a parish; no strangers were to be allowed to settle in a parish; and each parish was to be taxed for the relief of the poor. At the same time, every parish was to find something to do for all the poor who were able to work. Usually a stock of wool, hemp, and flax was bought, and the poor were supposed to be taught to spin. Each county was also to provide a House of Correction, where those who would not work should be forced to do so.

To keep down the number of poor people in a parish, order was given that only one family might live in one house, and no new house might be built in the country unless it had four acres of ground attached to it. In the cities of London and Westminster, and for three miles round them, no houses were to be built except for persons worth a specified amount. Houses might not be divided into tenements, nor might lodgers be taken in.

All this was to keep people as much as possible in the places where they belonged. The churchwardens and overseers had to attend to the relief of the poor. There are, belonging to a good many parishes in England, old account-books, showing how these officers raised and spent money on the relief of the poor. Some of these books go right back to this time, though most of them begin a good deal later. These officers had to keep a very sharp look-out. Of course they did not want the poor-rate to be any higher than they could help, so strangers coming into the parish were quickly tracked and hindered from gaining a settlement there. Vagabonds and strolling players were hurried out of the parish, and in some cases whipped. The stocks, the whipping-post, and the cage were set up near the church-yard gate, and they were in pretty constant use.

The officers were very anxious, too, to prevent any travellers from falling ill in their parish. Those who were sick, and could possibly be moved, they shifted on to the next parish, lest they should become chargeable to the parish. Some parishes spent a good deal of money, and the officers much time, in conveying people out of their bounds. That led, we may imagine, to many disputes between parishes, and gave the court of Quarter Sessions a lot of work to do; for amongst the many things which Quarter Sessions had to attend to was the carrying out of the Poor Laws.

Parishes had to look after and to support their own poor in much the same way right down to the early part of the nineteenth century, less than a hundred years ago.

Wayfarers, Early Fourteenth Century. From a manuscript in the British Museum.

The Moat House, Ightham, Kent. An example of a fortified manor house of feudal times. A large portion appears to be work of the fourteenth century (From an engraving published in 1845)

CHAPTER XXXVIII

Changes in Houses and House-building

In the time of King Edward III, that is, in the four-teenth century, there was a great change in the arrange-ment of castles and castle-building. We cannot say much about it here, it would take too long; but the changes made show that there was a desire to make the castle not merely a strong defence against an enemy, but also a dwelling-place for the baron, his family, his servants, and men-at-arms. Many buildings were added for comfort and convenience. In fact, a castle became a kind of little town.

William of Wykeham, that great master-builder, was

not only a builder of churches and colleges, but a castle-builder as well. The great Round Tower at Windsor Castle, and other parts of that building still in use, are his work; but in later times it has been much restored. The general arrangement of the Tower of London will give us an idea of the sort of habitation a castle of the fourteenth century was intended to be. In fact, we may say that every old castle, which is still inhabited, has considerable indications of work done in this and the following centuries, to fit it to be a comfortable dwelling-place as well as a fortress.

A good many houses, too, were protected by walls, and sometimes even called "castles", though they were not what we usually understand by the term. Many of these were moated houses, the moat forming the first line of protection. Then came the battlemented wall, within which the house proper was built.

The fourteenth and fifteenth centuries were stirring war times, and the nobles kept up bands of armed men, who lived close to, and even in, their strong houses and castles. In the fifteenth century, during the long period of the Wars of the Roses, there was much work for these "men-at-arms to do". This constant warfare weakened at length the power of the barons. Sometimes the Yorkist king, sometimes the Lancastrian king, was in power; and whichever side got the upper hand the king seized the property of the nobles on the other side.

As a matter of fact the nobles killed each other off, and when Henry Tudor, a Lancastrian, became king, there was an enormous amount of power in his hands; and he used it so as to keep a closer grip of it.

The towns and the traders had no liking for war, and they were quite satisfied to see the government of the country in the hands of a strong king. The new nobles, whom King Henry VII made, had most of them sprung from the merchant and trading class.

These new men, and even the king's own friends and supporters, were not allowed to keep bands of armed servants or retainers, able to turn the scale of a battle against the king. The Earl of Warwick, the " King-maker ", had played that game several times; and it was through Lord Stanley bringing his men over from King Richard III's side to the side of Henry in this way that he had won the Battle of Bosworth, and placed the English crown on Henry's head.

After becoming king, Henry VII determined that these bands of armed men, who would follow the whistle of their lord, must be put down. He therefore set to work cautiously, but he had his way. The nobles might no longer keep hosts of servants in livery as they pleased. The king cut down the numbers, so that he might be in a position to say to any of his nobles that his good word he did not want, and his bad word he cared nothing at all about.

You will remember the story of King Henry VII and the Earl of Oxford. The king went to pay the earl a visit, and his host, to show him honour, had two long lines of stout retainers, all armed and dressed in his livery, drawn up to meet him. He did all in his power to show honour to the king. When the visit was over, the king said to the earl:

" I thank you, my lord, for your good cheer, but I may not endure to have my laws broken in my sight; my attorney must speak with you."

Then there was "trouble"; and the earl thought himself very fortunate in getting out of the "scrape" by paying a small fine of ten thousand pounds. It was very awkward for a man to be a noble in Tudor times. He never knew exactly where he was. The king might be making a great fuss with him one day, clapping him in the Tower a few days after, and then chopping off his head and ornamenting London Bridge with it.

Well, this did away with the necessity for big fortified
houses which might contain barracks for soldiers, and
so we find that the new houses, built in Tudor times,
were less like fortresses than they had been before.
More attention was now paid to the size and convenience
of the rooms.   This sixteenth century was a great time
for the building of large houses; indeed, the new nobles
had better ideas of what a comfortable house was than
the older barons had.

Part of the House called Plas Mawr, Conway, Wales

*It illustrates the architectural change from the mediæval fortress to the Tudor
mansion which took place in the sixteenth century*

CHAPTER XXXIX

The Ruins of the Monasteries and the New Buildings

In early Tudor times our towns were much more picturesque than they are to-day. That was chiefly owing to the fact that there were in every town so many religious houses, colleges, and hospitals. These buildings all had grounds of their own in the town, some more, some less; but these open spaces and garden grounds, though they were not open to the public, all helped to make the town airy, and to give variety to the view.

The buildings themselves were all different, and many of them were hundreds of years old. Towers, spires, turrets, gables, gateways, and archways in all styles of architecture abounded. There were, of course, many things in the towns which we should not have liked, but they had a pleasant variety and picturesque appearance which our modern towns have not. Thousands of streets in our towns are just rows and rows of houses—brick boxes with slate lids—all alike, all ugly, and very dull and dreary to look at and to live in.

In the reign of King Henry VIII all the religious houses were suppressed, and given up into the king's hands. The life that had gone on in them for centuries came to an end. Both in town and country districts there were many people besides those who actually lived in them to whom this made a great difference—people who, in one way or another, got their living out of the monasteries. Shutting up the monasteries threw all these people, so to speak, out of work, and created what we call a " very difficult problem". That meant a great deal of suffering.

Nowadays, if a factory which has employed a number of people is suddenly closed, it means suffering for those who have been employed there and for their families. Now, though the monasteries did not employ people in the way in which a factory does, it did affect in many ways those who lived and worked and depended on them.

In these days, if people are thrown out of employment in one place they are free to go and seek it in another; but that was not the case in the reign of Henry VIII. If they wandered from their native towns and villages they were treated as vagabonds. It is true that the new persons, to whom the monastery lands were granted, were supposed to do for the people on the land—the poor and the sick—what the monasteries had done for them. But what they were *supposed* to do and what they *did do* were very different things.

It is pretty easy to see how things worked. A wealthy man managed to get a grant of the property of several monasteries at a very cheap rate. He did not want these places to live in; he wanted to make money out of them. The first thing that he did was to strip the buildings of everything which would fetch any money. The lead was usually the most valuable part of what the king had left. The roofs would be stripped, the graves broken open to get at the leaden coffins, and the windows smashed for the sake of the lead. Then the building was left standing a ruin. The poor people of the district had been used to receive food daily at the monastery gate, and no doubt had grumbled at the quality and quantity of the food often enough. But now it was no use going to the monastery gate, for the place was a ruin. They could not go to the new lord's house, for that might be miles away. Even if they did find him,

WOLLATON HALL, NOTTINGHAMSHIRE

An Elizabethan mansion, built 1590–1. The Italian style is here pervaded by a Gothic influence

he might be the owner of three or four such ruined monasteries. How could he be quite sure that they were the poor he was bound to relieve? And so the poor folk lost the daily food on which they had depended.

Then as regards the land. The new landlord, perhaps, might farm his fields; in which case the rents, instead of going to the monastery, went into his pocket. But he was not always on the spot, and very frequently the land was let out to tenants; an agent or steward collected the rents, and the tenants never saw their landlord. But many of these new owners found that the management of the estates caused them a lot of trouble; and, naturally enough, from their point of view, they wanted to get as much money out of the property as they could at the least cost to themselves.

Now there was in this sixteenth century still a great demand for wool, and many of these landlords found it would save trouble to turn these monastery lands into sheep-runs. A very few men could look after a great many sheep, and there would be no bother about keeping up buildings and barns. If the people were got off the land, there would be no poor to bother about relieving. So it came to pass that much land, which had been cultivated for many centuries, went out of cultivation, and the people were turned adrift. It was a hard state of affairs. The rights which they had had to relief from the religious houses were taken from them, and the means of getting their living also taken away; they were robbed of their employment, and punished for wandering, for not working, and for begging.

There were, of course, many instances in which the new landlord came and lived near the old monastery. In some cases the old buildings were altered and turned into a dwelling-house; in others the building material was used for building a brand-new house close by.

When this was the case the old custom of relieving the poor who came to the gate did not quickly die out.

For instance, at Standon in Hertfordshire, there was a house belonging to the Knights Hospitallers. When the house was dissolved, much of the property at Standon went to Sir Ralph Sadleir, who had been secretary to Thomas Cromwell, the "hammer of the monks". He owned Standon Lordship, and when the poor were no longer relieved at the Hospitallers' House in the village, they trooped from Standon up to Standon Lordship, about fifty of them, every day. That custom of relieving the poor was kept up there for many years.

Old Timbered House, at Presleigh, Radnorshire, dated 1616

CHAPTER XL

The New Houses of the Time of Queen Elizabeth

There were, in the days of Queen Elizabeth, in all parts of the country, hundreds of bare, gaunt ruins where once had been flourishing houses and centres of life and work. It may seem strange to us that the materials left were not sold and cleared away, and the sites made tidy. We must remember, however, that people could not build houses either in town or country as they chose. In Queen Elizabeth's reign the laws against building new houses were very strict indeed, so that there was not a very great demand for building material. Then, too, the quantity of such stone and wood in all these many buildings, in every town and almost every village, was enormous, so that the material was not worth much. The ruins were left, a sad and sorry sight, for many a long year.

In the towns some of the buildings were turned by their new owners into private houses, and the parts of the monastery were put to strange uses. Nobody seemed to mind; the spirit of destruction seemed to be in the air. Then, as years went on, and buildings needed repair, or roads wanted mending, the old ruins were the handiest places from which to get a load of stone; and so, with leave or without, many loads of stone were carted away from them.

We said just now that there was no encouragement given to the building of new houses in the reign of Queen Elizabeth, and yet most of the most picturesque old houses in our towns and villages still standing were built at that time. These, however, were not new houses; they were rebuilt on old sites, *improved* according to the ideas of the time.

Moreton Old Hall, Cheshire, built 1550–59. An example of the half-timbered Elizabethan house for which Cheshire and Shropshire are specially famous

You will notice in country places a great many houses built somewhat after this style. Many of them are now cottages, but they were not built for cottages; they were the ordinary houses in which yeomen lived in the sixteenth century.

There was the hall or house-place—an oblong room in the centre—on to which other rooms were built, forming a wing at one end, or often a wing at each end, with gables towards the street, and projecting upper stories. A great deal might be said about this kind of house, but there is only space for a very short account of it.

The house was built upon a foundation of stone or brick, so that the wooden sill should be above the ground-level. Into this wooden sill strong upright posts of timber, quite rough, some eight or nine inches square, were set. The posts at the angles were larger, often being butts of trees placed roots upwards, so that the upper story might project. Then on the main posts beams were laid, the ends projecting, upon which the framing of the upper story was set. It was just a timber skeleton, into which other timbers were set eight or nine inches apart. In later times these timbers were wider apart, and curved or diagonal braces were often used, but at first the uprights were pretty closely set.

The spaces between the uprights were then filled in with lath and plaster, flush with the woodwork. In some parts of the country brick was used instead, set in herring-bone fashion. In later times, when the lath and plaster had decayed, the spaces were often filled in with brickwork laid in the ordinary way. Then again, in other cases the woodwork of the house shrank and left gaps between the lath and plaster and the wood, so the whole of the outside has been covered with plaster, or weather-boarded and painted or tarred, or hung over with tiles.

The windows were small, and sometimes in the upper story one was built out, forming an oriel. The roofs were high pitched, in many cases tiled, but more often thatched. In these old houses the chimney-stack is a great feature outside, and the huge fireplace, with its wide chimney-corners, takes up half the house-place inside. From most of these nowadays the old hearth is gone, and a small chimney-breast has been bricked up to take a modern range; but the old chimney-corner, with its funny little window, can usually still be traced.

There are quite a large number of village inns of this kind. Very often these are the oldest and most picturesque buildings left in a village, except the church. It is these old-fashioned houses which make village scenery so pleasing to the eye after the dreary rows of bunches of brick, with holes in them for windows, covered in with slate, which fill the streets of our towns, all alike, and all ugly.

CHAPTER XLI

Larger Elizabethan and Jacobean Houses

We have said that the Tudor period was a time of building of big houses and mansions. Every county in England has some such houses to show. Many of them were built of stone, some partly of brick and stone. Their style shows that the English or old fashion of Gothic building was dying out. Italian ideas and Italian ornament were coming into favour. No doubt one reason why so much of the old work was ruthlessly destroyed was because it was out of fashion. It is astonishing, even in these days, how much good work is destroyed just because it has gone out of date. Among the most famous of these houses we may mention Burleigh House "by Stamford Town", Haddon Hall, and Knebworth; and, belonging to a rather later date, Hatfield House.

For a big house the idea was to build it round a quadrangle. Smaller houses were in plan very like the half-timbered houses of the yeomen, only on a larger scale, and more richly ornamented. The hall and its wings were extended considerably, and, with a handsome porch, formed in plan a big capital E, thus:—

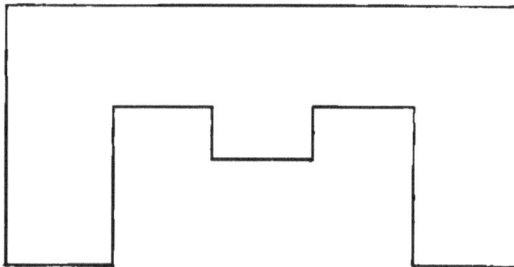

Hall and Staircase, Knole House, Kent, 1570. The broad heavily-carved staircase of oak was a special feature of Elizabethan houses

Some people have thought that this plan was chosen in honour of Queen Elizabeth, but the truth is that it was the most convenient form, and fitted in best with the ideas of the time. It had grown up quite naturally, in the course of many generations, from the simple hall with the hearth in the middle, the beginnings of which we saw in the huts of the pit-dwellers.

Quite early in the fourteenth century brick had begun to come into use for building, but the first bricks were probably imported from Flanders. Hull, which had been founded by King Edward I, had many buildings of brick, and by about the year 1320 it had brick-yards of its own. Flemish weavers were encouraged to settle in England by King Edward III, and they used brick in buildings which they set up. There are a good

CHAS WADE.

A Room in an Elizabethan House. A reconstruction, in the Victoria and Albert Museum, London, of panelling and furniture removed from a house at Bromley by Bow, London

many houses in the eastern counties and in Kent still standing, which show Flemish and Dutch ideas.

Cardinal Wolsey's palace at Hampton Court is a good specimen of the brickwork of his time; and all through the reign of King Henry VIII the chief material used was brick, terra-cotta[1] being employed for mouldings and ornament. This was chiefly the work of Italian artists, and they produced also some very beautiful ceilings in plaster-work[2] for many of their fine houses.

After King Henry VIII's quarrel with Rome fewer Italians were employed, and English artists were left to work out these new ideas in their own way. From about the middle of the sixteenth century the use of terra-cotta dropped out, and moulded and shaped bricks began to be used, though stone was used for the more ornamental portions.

When we reach the reign of King James I, we find that the leading architect was Inigo Jones. We do not hear very much of architects during the Middle Ages. The man employed to do the actual work was allowed to select his own materials and carry out his own ideas pretty much in his own way. But in the sixteenth century the architect became a more important person than the craftsman, and the craftsman had to work according to the pattern and design provided for him.

The Jacobean[3] houses show that the old English styles of building were being left behind, and a newer type of house, plainer and heavier, was taking its place. The Civil War was a very bad time for architects and craftsmen, but after the Restoration a better time came to them again.

The Great Fire of London, which swept away almost

---

[1] *Terra-cotta* is a compound of pure clay, fine sand, or powdered flint.
[2] See the picture on p. 144.
[3] *Jacobean* means of the time of James I and on to James II.

every mediæval building in the city, gave a great
impetus, or push forward, to building. You can quite
understand that, with so much building going on, the
work would be somewhat hurried and very much
plainer than it had been. So London became a city
of bricks and mortar. Middlesex has large quantities
of good brick-earth; and though bricks were made in
that county long before the Great Fire, the Great Fire
developed the industry greatly. There was a worthy
old Royalist knight of Hammersmith, Sir Nicholas
Crispe, who, after the execution of King Charles I, went
over to Holland, as so many other Royalists did. There
he watched very closely bricks and brick-making, and
when he came back to England he introduced many
improvements in the art of brick-making along the
Thames valley.

*Blickling Hall, Norfolk, built 1619. Illustrates the typical features of a
Jacobean Mansion*

CHAPTER XLII

Churches after the Reformation

Not very long after the dissolution of the monasteries the churches had a very bad time to go through. It is perfectly marvellous how rapidly some people, who were in power, discovered that the valuable ornaments and fittings in them were so very wicked and superstitious, that the only thing to do was to seize them for the use of the king as his private property. No attempt was made to apply the money taken for the benefit of the parishes; it was shamefully and shamelessly squandered. The buildings were very badly treated, and everything in some of them that could be defaced and destroyed was so treated. The changes made in religion under the Tudor kings and queens were so many, and so violent, that ordinary everyday people could not understand them, and deeply religious people were driven in opposite directions. There was bitter persecution for all who did not fall in with the will of the Tudor sovereign, whether Catholic or Protestant, and good men had to suffer and to die on both sides for their faith.

All who did not attend their parish church, and take part in the services which those in authority considered to be most fitting, were regarded as bad citizens, and treated as such. We cannot wonder that the parish churches were allowed to go to decay. English people had spent much money on their churches right up to the time of the Reformation. Then they saw the gifts they and their forefathers had made abused or stolen. People were not disposed to do much for their churches after that. In some cases, especially in country places where the leading people were Catholics or Puritans,

Monument in Chelsea Church, London; date about 1630

it seems as if they purposely let the parish church, to which they were compelled to go by law, get so thoroughly out of order that they might be able to say there was no church to go to.

Many of the houses built during Tudor times had secret chambers and hiding-places, which were known only to a very few persons. And such hiding-places were much used, in the times of Queen Elizabeth and King James I, by priests, who ministered in secret to those who clung to the old faith.

But though the churches were much out of repair, in some of them stately and costly monuments were erected in the sixteenth and early part of the seventeenth centuries. They were different from the monuments set up before the Reformation, and were usually built against a wall. They were of various coloured marbles, the effigies lying under circular-headed canopies, supported by columns in the Italian style. The effigies of man and wife were usually represented clad in robes of state, coloured, their children kneeling round the tomb in various attitudes.

By and by, instead of the effigies being represented as lying on their backs, with hands clasped, they were shown lying on one side, supporting their heads on their hands. There are many such monuments, for instance, in Westminster Abbey, and in almost every old town church one or more can be seen.

It became a very common practice for one of the old chapels, built on to the parish church in mediæval times, to be set apart as the private burial-place of a great landowner. Many new chapels were built for this special purpose. In them we may see specimens of the different fashions in monuments from Tudor days, or earlier, right down to the present time.

CHAPTER XLIII

Building after the Restoration: Houses

The most notable architect after the Great Fire of London was Sir Christopher Wren, and his master-piece is, of course, St. Paul's Cathedral. He designed, too, most of the city churches. The style was adopted in various parts of the country by various noblemen for building great houses. Brick was regarded as too mean a material for such very grand houses, and stone was used for facing them.

In the houses which Wren built brick was very largely

House at Rainham, Essex, built during the reign of Queen Anne

used. He introduced rubbed bricks, and had them laid
with very close joints. We have some very fine examples
of such brickwork in gables of various forms in the early
part of the eighteenth century—the reign of Queen Anne.

Designs for houses did not improve in beauty as the
eighteenth century went on. Many of the houses were
very substantially built, and were arranged with an eye
to comfort and convenience. The hall, which had been
the centre of the old English home, became smaller and
smaller; the kitchens were placed below the ground-level,
and in towns were often reached by a flight of steps down
from the street to the area, which is still so common in
London streets.

The front door of the house became the great ornamental feature of the building, approached by a flight of steps often protected by very handsome iron railings. Attached to many of the railings still are light upright posts for carrying an old-fashioned oil-lamp. Just a few of these lamp-carriers have extinguishers, which were for the use of the link-boys, when on dark nights they had safely lighted the master of the house through the dangers of the streets to his own front door.

The brickwork of these houses had become very plain, and less and less stone was used for ornament—a little over the principal windows, and the boldly cut quoins at the angles of the house. Most of the windows were merely oblong openings in the blank wall.

The great point aimed at was to get a handsome doorway. Sometimes a portico was built out, supported by stone pillars having richly-carved capitals. In other cases a canopy, supported by half-columns, or by brackets, was placed over the doorway. Stone was sometimes used for these canopies, but wood was more common. These wooden canopies and brackets are often very fine pieces of joinery and wood-carving. The canopy sometimes takes the form of a kind of big shell, the ornaments and pattern being finely moulded, and the cornice being deeply and boldly cut. These canopies were painted, and the tops covered with lead to protect them from the weather. As you walk along streets of an old town, which has not been too much modernized, you will be almost sure to see some specimens of this kind of work.

The thick panelled doors of these houses are often grand pieces of work, which would rejoice the heart of a joiner who loves his craft. So many boys now are taught something of joinery at school that there must be a good many of them who know enough to see the beauty there is in a good piece of work, even though it may be quite plain.

Another feature in these doorways is the window over the door, intended to give light to the hall. We call it the fan-light, because it was usually made somewhat in the shape of an open fan, and you will find in fan-lights some very pretty designs cleverly put together.

About the middle of the eighteenth century stucco came into fashion. It was easy to handle, and ornamental patterns could be readily produced. The ornamental stone and woodwork was imitated in plaster. Like all mere imitations of good work, it soon became poor, and showed itself to be a sham; but it was very fashionable. There was such a rage for it that the brickwork of a house was often covered with a smooth coat of it, and the whole painted white, or cream colour. Some of the old houses of good sound brick were covered in this way, and it was often used to cover up very poor bricks and brickwork. Good plaster-work, no doubt, often served a purpose in keeping out damp, but it was very formal, and not very beautiful.

Doorway from a House in Gt. Ormond Street, London, now in the
Victoria and Albert Museum, London

In the middle of the same century a fancy for Gothic architecture revived, and many brick buildings were built with pointed arches, doorways, and windows, with turrets and pinnacles, all covered with plaster-work and cement, imitating Gothic mouldings and carvings; but it was only sham Gothic, and not at all satisfactory.

Indeed, we may say that, as the century went on, houses did not become more beautiful. As the population increased in the town, streets of houses sprang up, some large, some small, built in rows and crescents and terraces, in which all the houses were alike; and very dull and drab and mean-looking many of them have become. When they were built they were made to look neat, or even smart, in front, but little care was taken about the appearance and convenience of their backs. They were not arranged in such a way that each might have a proper amount of light, and that a free current of air could pass through them and around them.

In some respects we have improved our houses, but we have much to learn yet. We have, for instance, yet to see that *all* our houses, however small, shall have a proper number of bedrooms, large, light, and airy—for we spend one-third of our lives in them. We have also to see that both beauty and fitness shall be properly considered in building a house. Too often no care is taken to provide proper places where food and clothing can be kept, and where that very necessary but unpleasant process of washing and drying of clothes can be carried on without spoiling the comfort and health of the household. Every house needs a bathroom of some sort, as much as a grate; for where dirt is there is disease, suffering, and death. We are thinking very much in these days about the absolute need for better housing of the people; indeed, that is one of the " big problems " which we have to tackle.

CHAPTER XLIV

Building after the Restoration: Churches

After the Reformation the churches, as we have said, were much neglected for a long time. They were used in a different way from what they had been in the Middle Ages—a great deal more was thought of preaching and hearing sermons. People grew to be very particular as to where they sat in church, and to have a seat in accordance with their dignity and importance. Pews became very important things. Churches were not heated in those days, though the services were very long, for sermons often lasted for an hour or two. No doubt one reason for making pews so high was to keep off draughts. The great people of the parish seemed to try to outdo each other in the height of their pews. Some of the grand pews had canopies to them, like old-fashioned four-post bedsteads, and they were hung round with curtains. In later times they even had fire-places, with "poker, tongs, and shovel" all complete.

Gradually the whole floor-space got filled up with pews with high wooden walls, some square, some oblong, all shut in with doors, and with seats running round them. A little girl who was once taken to a church which was fitted with these "horse-box" pews, when she came home told her mother: "We went into a cupboard and sat on a shelf!" The fashion of having pews shut in with doors lasted for several centuries; indeed you may see them still in some churches, though they are not nearly as high as they once were.

The churches needed repairs from time to time in the seventeenth century, and a few, a very few, new ones were built. But money was not spent upon them as it had been in the Middle Ages. They were patched up

Pews in a Church at Stokesay, Shropshire, rebuilt 1654

and mended for the most part as cheaply as possible. In very few cases was any attempt made to make them as beautiful as the houses which were being built at the time.

After the Restoration there arose a great interest in bells and bell-ringing. At the end of the seventeenth century a great many rings of bells were hung in the old steeples and belfries, which had to be altered to receive them.

The monuments set up in the churches in the reign of King Charles II were somewhat smaller than they had been. They were often tablets on the walls, ornamented with curious carvings of skulls and cross-bones, cherubs' heads, curtains, and festoons of flowers and fruits, often finely carved. You will not find in churchyards many grave-stones or tombs of an earlier date than 1660. The head-stones were then very small, and had little on them except "Here lyeth the body of" so-and-so, and the date.

A great many churches were built in London after the Fire. They were furnished with high pews, usually all of the same height, and having doors. The wood-work, especially of the pulpit, reading-desk, and organ-case, in these churches is mostly very fine. A celebrated carver of this period was Grinling Gibbons, and he and his pupils did a great deal of such work, both in churches and houses.

In other parts of the country Wren's work was imitated in some of the new churches then built, and in some of the old ones which were altered or rearranged. One of the best specimens of work done at this time is to be seen in Whitchurch, in Middlesex.

Not very many new churches, however, were built until the beginning of the nineteenth century, except in some of the towns which had grown up from country villages. In and round London most of the villages increased so much in size that the little old parish church was much too small for the population. Galleries were put up in them in all sorts of queer places, to provide more seats. More room still being wanted, many churches were pulled down, and larger buildings set up.

The new churches of the latter part of the eighteenth and the early years of the nineteenth centuries were simply big oblong rooms. The outsides were often copies of parts of Grecian temples. They were crowned with towers and spires somewhat like those on Wren's churches, but not nearly so handsome.

Inside, the church was fitted up with a gallery running along two sides and across one end. In the end gallery a big organ was placed, and on either side of it, high

INTERIOR OF ST. MARY-LE-BOW, LONDON

up, near the ceiling, were smaller galleries, one for the charity-school boys, the other for the charity-school girls of the parish. The galleries and floor of the church were filled with high pews. On the floor opposite the organ were three huge boxes, rising one above the other. The lowest box was for the parish clerk, the middle one was the reading-desk, and the highest was the pulpit, which was often provided with a sounding-board, not unlike an umbrella. The altar was in a little niche behind the pulpit. Chapels were fitted up in much the same way.

Under all these churches and chapels were vaults, in which people were buried, but not in the earth. The coffins were placed on shelves, one above the other, round the vault. On the walls of the church above were often tablets to the memory of people lying in the vaults below. These, by the nineteenth century, were for the most part simply slabs of white marble, with black or grey borders. There was hardly any carving at all on them; only inscriptions or epitaphs, and texts.

The churchyards were used for burials, and by the middle of the nineteenth century most of them were crowded with tombstones. In London nearly all are now laid out in open spaces; many of the gravestones have quite disappeared, and those which remain are rapidly perishing.

When we remember that the churchyards of the old churches had been used as burial-places in many cases since the early days of Christianity, and even before that, we can easily grasp the fact that the earth had been used over and over again for burials. About the middle of the nineteenth century the nation came to the conclusion that burials in churches and crowded town churchyards should no longer be allowed. The practice was dangerous to the living. So cemeteries were opened in districts away from the towns and homes

of the people. Towns have grown so fast that many of
these cemeteries are now surrounded by houses, and in
the midst of big populations.

About the year 1840 interest began to be taken in the
old English styles of building, and a taste for Gothic
architecture arose again. Since that time places of
worship of all descriptions have for the most part been
built in some sort of Gothic. When you read that such
and such a church or building is in the fourteenth- or
fifteenth-century style, you must understand that it is
not a copy of a church built in the fourteenth or fifteenth
century, but that its window-heads, doorways, arches,
and fittings are *in the style* of the fourteenth or fifteenth
century. Most of these modern buildings are of brick,
only faced or dressed with stone. It is pretty safe to say
that there is no old church standing which was built
entirely in the fourteenth century, and has remained
unaltered from that day to this. Nearly all the old
churches have been restored, a good many of them
several times during the last sixty or seventy years.
Unfortunately, through ignorance, a good many interesting features in the old buildings were swept away during
these "restorations". An old building needs very careful handling when we set about repairing it.

In our towns almost every tower and spire which we
see is a modern building, though the *styles* may vary
from Norman to Perpendicular and seventeenth century.
Modern buildings, churches, halls, public offices, and
private houses are mostly imitations of the work of past
ages. There is no nineteenth-century style of English
architecture. Some day, perhaps, England may develop
a new style of architecture, such as the world has never
yet seen, but at the present time we seem to be only able
to copy and adapt the work of those who have gone
before us.

King Edward VI's School and Alms Houses, Stratford-on-Avon

CHAPTER XLV

Schools after the Reformation

A little of the property which had belonged to the religious houses was saved and turned to useful purposes. Just a very few of the old alms-houses were allowed to continue their work, like St. Cross at Winchester, and some schools and colleges were founded.

There are quite a number of such schools which bear the name of King Edward the Sixth. But Edward VI was only a lad of sixteen when he died, and he had practically nothing to do with either the good or the evil which was done in his name. In other towns besides London, good men set to work and managed to get grants of some small parts of the property of old religious houses, and adapted them for school work. In some instances they were allowed to have part of an old ruin, which they patched up and turned into a schoolroom, and some of these queer old rooms continued in use for many generations. At St. Alban's the lady chapel at the east end of the Abbey Church was walled off from the main building in the time of Edward VI, and from that time it was used as the Grammar School until about a third of a century ago.

It is quite true to say that a good number of our present grammar-schools rose out of the ashes of the monasteries. But they were not great buildings intended for hundreds of scholars. Many of them were founded for ten or a dozen scholars drawn from a particular town or district. The sum set apart for the upkeep of the schools was usually very small, and not always readily forthcoming. The master was always a man who had taken a degree at one of the universities, but his salary was so small that he had to engage in other work as well in order to make a living. If he was an enthusiastic teacher, in some cases he attracted scholars from outside, who were not on the foundation, from whom he got fees, and in this way he increased his income, and was able to make a living. Some schools had an usher as well as the master; and at times when the number of scholars was very small they were left to the usher, the master devoting his time to other work, and only drawing the salary due to him. In such cases the school fell to a low ebb, the number of scholars dwindled, and the buildings were allowed to fall to decay. All of them had their ups and downs; at times doing good work, at others doing very little at all. That went on for many years. However, most of them are alive and active to-day, and many of them have histories of which they may be proud, and a past which should help them to excel in the future.

Children were often taught in the church and church

porch in country places. John Evelyn was so taught in the early part of the seventeenth century, and many more people could read and write than we sometimes imagine; but knowledge was not within the reach of all.

The condition of the poor occupied a good deal of attention, and the poor laws were used to improve matters in many ways. At Norwich, for instance, in the year 1632, a children's hospital was provided for boys between the ages of ten and fourteen. They were to be taught useful trades, and fed and clothed. For dinner they were to have six ounces of bread, one pint of beer, and, on three days of the week, one pint of pottage and six ounces of beef; on the four other days, one ounce of butter and two ounces of cheese. For supper they were to have six ounces of bread, one pint of beer, one ounce of butter, and two ounces of cheese. For breakfast every day they had three ounces of bread, half an ounce of butter, and a half-pint of beer.

About the year 1686 the Middlesex magistrates established what they called a "College for Infants". This is what they said about their plan:—

"The Justices, having observed great inconveniences from the loose upbringing of parish children whereby very few of them come to good. Order made that a great part of the Corporation House is fitted up for that purpose, and excellent rules and methods are therein taken for their education in true religion and virtue. Order made for the parishes to send fifty children in all."

Towards the end of the seventeenth century, and in the early part of the eighteenth century, we find another sort of school coming into existence—the charity-schools. These were intended to give a simpler sort of education than that which the grammar-schools were supposed to give. They were intended for what was called the poorer classes. Now in the grammar-schools it was essential that the master should be a man of some

*Charity School, Gravel Lane, London.   From a print published in 1819.
The school was opened in 1687*

learning and standing—he must have taken a degree
at one of the universities.   But in these charity-schools
it was not thought to be essential that the teacher should
have both learning and the ability to teach.   They were
managed by governors, who drew up rules and regulations as to what was to be done in the schools, and it
was the teacher's business just to carry out these regulations as best he could.   So there was much learning
by rote.   There was reading, in which the Bible was
the chief, sometimes the only, reading-book, a certain
amount of writing, and a little arithmetic.   Where the
master happened to be a person of ability, some good
work was done.   Writing was often very carefully and
thoroughly taught, and the handwriting was far in

advance of most of the abominable stuff which we scribble in these days and make do duty for writing. The girls were taught needlework, and had to spend long hours every day at the task. It is very interesting to read through the old order-books kept by the governors of these old-fashioned schools, and to glean from them something of the daily life in these humble schools. The rules and regulations made from time to time seem to us very strange and even ridiculous, and it is a very easy matter to make fun out of them. But we must remember that at the time they were drawn up the worthy governors had very good reasons for what they did, and we cannot but honour them for doing their best according to their lights. There were charity-schools in almost every town and in a good many villages; some founded by bodies of men, others by private individuals. The buildings varied according to the amount of money which the governors had to spend upon them. Some are very picturesque buildings. For instance, there is the Dewhurst School at Cheshunt, founded in 1640, and Mrs. Lucie Fuller's School at Watford, founded in 1704.

The scholars of these schools attended daily, on Sundays as well as workdays. On Sundays and some other days they were all marched off to church, where they sat in dreadful little galleries built mostly high up in dark corners on either side of the organ. These charity-schools were carried on in much the same way right down to the middle of the nineteenth century. The scholars were mostly dressed in the costume of the period at which the school was founded; and very quaint and curious they looked. Almost the last link now left of such dress is that in which a "Bluecoat Boy" may still be seen. That dress is a relic of the dress worn in the middle of the sixteenth century. The little charity-school boys wore leather breeches—which in later times were altered mostly to corduroy—coloured stockings; coats of a quaint cut with funny little tails at the back, of brown or green or grey or black cloth, and round, flat caps in colours to match their coats; pewter or brass badges on their breasts, bearing the name or device or the arms of the school, and two little pieces of fine linen fluttering under their chins, called "bands". This was the ordinary boys' dress in the eighteenth century, and the charity-school boys continued to wear it long after it had gone out of fashion. The charity-school girls had frocks and cloaks of a wonderful cut, in colours corresponding with the boys' coats; white tippets, aprons, and "such mob caps". In church they led the singing, what little there was, and their hours in school were long, very long, but they found time to get in a fair amount of play, and had plenty of time for getting into mischief as the order-books of the governors bear witness.

People often laugh at these old-fashioned charity-schools and speak of them with contempt. That is absolutely a wrong thing to do, because they were founded many years before Parliament troubled itself about the education of the people. We cannot too greatly honour those worthy old-fashioned men and women who did what they could to provide some teaching and training for poor boys and girls, and to put them in the way of earning their own living.

By the end of the eighteenth century people were beginning to be concerned at the ignorance of the great masses of the people in this country, and we find that in a good many places little schools were being kept, taught by the parish

Bluecoat Boy

A SCHOOL PLAYGROUND SCENE

From the painting, "The Fight Interrupted" (1815), by William Mulready, R.A., in the Victoria and Albert Museum, South Kensington, London

.

clerk or by some old lady; and here and there we find attempts being made to form parish schools. These were for the most part on the same lines as the older charity-schools, but maintained by subscriptions from private persons.

In the first year of the nineteenth century, Joseph Lancaster, a member of the Society of Friends, took over a big disused barn in the Borough Road, London, and set up this inscription over the door:—

"All who wish may send their children and have them educated freely; and those who do not wish to have their education for nothing may pay for it if they please."

He tried to teach, and keep in order, several hundred children at the same time. He had them arranged in little classes of seven or eight children spelling out verses from the Bible, printed on large cards, under the guidance of an older child. Groups of these little classes were under the charge of an older child still, called a superintendent. Writing was taught in little classes, the children tracing the forms of the letters in sand, strewn on flat benches. Everything was regulated by rule, and done at words of command, given by the head teacher.

A few years later, a churchman, Dr. Bell, started a somewhat similar method of instruction, by means of monitors, which he had tried in Madras some thirty years before.

Those were the beginnings of the primary schools of to-day. From Lancaster's work there sprang a society, called the "British and Foreign School Society", and from Bell's work another, known as the "National Society". These two societies set to work vigorously to see what they could do to improve education and to promote the building of schools. They very soon found that the great need was for teachers, trained for

Schoolmaster and Pupils, early Seventeenth Century. From a woodcut published in 1631

this special work—folk who not only had knowledge as to *what* to teach, but also who had been trained *how* to teach. That was the beginning of a new order of teachers, and Training Colleges for Teachers was the outcome of their efforts. These private societies led the way in the face of much opposition; for there were hosts of people who "didn't see why" there should be all this fuss about the education of the masses of the people. At last, after much difficulty, in the year 1833, Parliament made a grant of twenty thousand pounds to these two societies, to be used by them in the work of building schools. That was the beginning of State Grants for Education.

Then in various parts of the country people were stirred to build schools, aided by grants and advice of these societies; and that was the beginning of our modern schoolrooms. In 1839 Parliament really took in hand the work of Education, and Inspectors of Schools were appointed, and the Education Department set up to look after the work of Education in the country. Much was left for private individuals to do; but, from that time, the work has gone forward slowly, and the State has taken a greater part in the work. In 1870 a great step forward was taken, and again and again since then things have moved onward; and at last, in 1918, another Education Act was passed which aims at making the Education of the Nation more than it has ever yet been one of the very first duties of the State.

The school buildings which the two societies set on foot in the course of time have become unsuitable for the work to be done in them, and changes have had to take place. Since 1870 a very large number of new school buildings have been erected; but changing times already call for many alterations to suit them for the fresh methods of carrying on the work in the best interests of those who have to be taught in them. So many things have to be considered now of which we knew but very little in the days gone by, and we can never sit down and say that the work is complete, and that no more improvements can be made.

Richmond County School. A modern council school under the supervision of the Board of Education

CHAPTER XLVI

Apprentices

From many of these old-fashioned schools boys and girls were apprenticed. Connected with old parishes there are still funds for placing out boys and girls to trades and crafts. All through the Middle Ages, and right on into modern times, children were set to work when quite young, and it was a common custom to send them away from home for this purpose. The children of the upper classes, the boys especially, were trained in the households of other nobles and squires. The idea was to bring them up "hardy", though to us it seems a somewhat unnatural way of doing it. An Italian, who visited England about the year 1500, was much struck by this English custom, and he did not at all approve of such young children being given over to the bringing up by strangers. Both boys and girls from quite well-to-do homes were very often thus sent out, when they were between seven and nine years of age, and apprenticed for seven or nine years, not only to learn some trade or craft, but to private houses where they were set to do menial and drudging work of all sorts. The idea was "that they might learn better manners" than they would do at home. In many wealthy homes it is still the practice to send boys to boarding-school when they reach ten years of age for the greater part of each year, away from home and home influence, before they are sent on to a public school and, later, to a university.

All through the Middle Ages the only way by which a man could become a craftsman was by being first of all an apprentice, and the rules by which a lad was bound to a master were very strict. Things did not alter much in this respect in the sixteenth, seventeenth, and eighteenth centuries. An apprentice was always bound for seven years in the presence of magistrates. The master had to find his apprentice in food, clothing, lodging, and to instruct him in his art, or "mystery" as it was called. The apprentice lived in his master's house, and was bound to serve him.

His master could chastise him if he was idle or "saucy", and even have him sent to the house of correction for further punishment. Both masters and apprentices could complain of each other to the magistrates at the Quarter Sessions, and the hearing of the complaints often took up a lot of time. According to many of the complaints, of which records still exist, some of the apprentices must have had rather a hard time—"seven years, hard". Some complained of having to eat mouldy cheese and rotten meat; others, of their ragged clothes; others, that their masters beat them with pokers, hammers, pint-pots, to say nothing of whips and sticks; prevented them from going to church; and others, that their masters turned them out of doors, or ran away and left them. The masters, on their side, often complain that their apprentices are idle, that they rob them, that they stop out at night and keep company with bad characters, and so on. So it seems they did not always get on well together.

But then there were the others—those who made the best of it. Where the master did his duty, and

Apprentice, Sixteenth Century. From a contemporary woodcut

the apprentice took pains to learn, they got on pretty well together. It was not an easy life for the apprentice, but it made him a craftsman.

The children of those who belonged to the poorer classes were apprenticed to unskilled occupations in a similar way, and if the parents neglected to do this the parish authorities interfered and found places and masters for them.

In some parts of the country there were little schools where children were taught straw-plait and lace-making. Some of these lasted right down to days which people still living can remember, in Hertfordshire and Bedfordshire.

Apprentices, Eighteenth Century. Two apprentices at the looms of their master, a silk-weaver of Spitalfields, London. A striking contrast in industry and idleness. After an engraving by Hogarth published in 1787

CHAPTER XLVII

Play

In all the many centuries of our history there have been boys and girls; and, whatever has been going on in the world around them, they have found time to play. In the Great War our soldiers could not but be struck by the way in which the children in places under bombardment took advantage of any lull in the firing to come out of their hiding places, and go on with their games, in spite of the ruin and desolation and danger all round them.

Many of our English games go back so far in the history of man that their origin is forgotten. Yet there are games which children play now just as they did in the days of Queen Elizabeth; and those queer rhymes, which you know so well, and understand nothing about, have been repeated, some of them, since England began to be England.

There is plenty to say about games, but not enough space to say it all here. There are some games which come and go as regularly as the seasons. The queer part of it all is: Who starts the game? As sure as the early spring evenings arrive you will find boys playing at marbles. Town or country, it does not matter, all at once "marbles are *in*". Nobody says it is "marble season"; nobody ever yet found the boy who brings out the first marble of the season. Somehow a *something* inside a boy tells him it is "marble" time, and the marbles appear in his pocket.

It is just the same with "tops"; they come and they go with absolute regularity. They come as if by magic, and by magic they disappear. When the errand-boy, who has left school a month or two, stops, basket on arm, to watch the game, you may be sure that it is the height of the season. When the ground is occupied by the little chaps who have just come up from the infant school, and the errand-boy passes whistling by on the other side, it is quite certain that the season is over and gone.

These are games that want no clubs, associations, nor subscriptions. Yet they are governed by time-honoured rules, which have never been written down, but must be strictly observed, or there is much talking and wrangling over the game.

Sports have an important place in the life of towns and villages nowadays; but, though cricket and football are old games really, they have not always been as popular as they are now. Cricket, in some form or other, was played in the thirteenth century when it was played with a crooked or clubbed stick called a "cryc". Indeed all games where a ball is used are more or less ancient. It seems to have been played at Guildford as early as 1598, but modern cricket only dates from the middle of the eighteenth century. Kent seems to have led the way, and Hampshire was the home of the game in 1774.

Tennis, or "fives" was a favourite game for many centuries, and it was quite a common thing in some places for it to be played against the church tower, which was a very convenient

The Game of Bob-apple, Fourteenth Century.
From an illustration in a manuscript in the British Museum

CRICKET, EIGHTEENTH CENTURY

After a painting made in 1745 by Francis Hayman, R.A.

Boys' Sports. From a woodcut published in 1659

1, *Bowling stones.* 2, *Throwing a bowl at nine pins, 3.* 4, *Striking a ball through a ring, 5, with a bandy.* 6, *Scourging a top with a whip, 7.* 8, *Shooting with a " trunck" or a bow, 9.* 10, *Going on stilts.* 11, *Tossing and swinging on a " merry-totten".*

place for the game. Complaints were frequently made of the damage done to and around the churches by the playing of unlawful and disordered games of many kinds. At times attempts were made to put down the playing of tennis. But by the time of Queen Elizabeth it had come into favour, and the privilege of keeping tennis-courts was eagerly sought for, and the game became very popular indeed later on; but it went out of fashion again towards the end of the eighteenth century, only to be revived again in our own times.

It is only within the last forty years that football has become popular. Football of some kind has been played for many centuries, especially in the streets of towns. Kingston, Chester, and Dorking, amongst other

places, have a custom of playing football on Shrove
Tuesday. The story as to how the custom arose is
the same in most of these places.

Far back in the ninth century a party of Danes
ravaged the district and attacked the town. The townsmen made a brave stand against them till help came.
Then the Danes were defeated, their· leader slain, his
head struck off, and kicked about the streets in triumph.
That is said to have given rise to the custom; but it
was a very ghastly football.

Football was not always regarded with favour. Folk
often wanted to play football when their lords and masters
wanted them to practise shooting with their bows and
arrows; but they were frequently told what a dangerous
game it was, and over and over again it was forbidden.
Football was always apparently a game over which the
players fell out, much as they do now. Nearly four hundred years ago a worthy gentleman wrote of the game :—

"It is nothyng but beastely fury and extreme violence,
whereby procedeth hurte, and consequently rancour and
malice do remayne with thym that be wounded ".

There are some places where the schoolboys of long,
long ago have left their marks. In the cloisters at Westminster Abbey, at Canterbury, at Norwich, at Salisbury
and at Gloucester Cathedral, for instance, are some roughly
cut marks in the old benches, forming the
"tables" or "boards" on which they played
some almost forgotten games with stones.

Then, too, there is "hop-scotch" which at
some seasons of the year makes the side-
walks of many bye-streets so untidy with
its rudely chalked courts; rounders and
"tip-cat"; battledore and shuttlecock, to
say nothing of skipping and many another
game—all old, old games, which are ever
new, and never out of date.

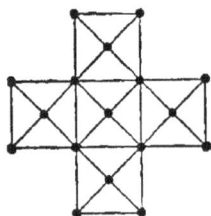

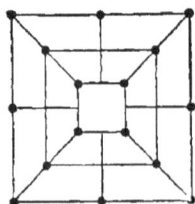

CHAPTER XLVIII

Roads

All roads lead to London and have done so for many a century, and so we find, as we should expect to do, that roads from all parts of the country converge towards it like the spokes of a wheel to its centre. The same sort of thing is seen in all towns of any size. Cross roads connect these main roads, and the nearer we are to the town the greater is the number of these, and they are often as busy and as important as the old main roads. But as we get away from the towns into the more rural districts, the lesser roads which connect the villages and hamlets with each other become fewer, more winding and straggling. There are also green lanes and field paths, and it is by following these, rather than the high roads, that the real beauties of the country can be seen. A person dashing along the main road in a motor-car, on a motor-cycle or a bicycle misses much which a man on foot, who is not in a tremendous hurry, is able to see and enjoy.

Not very long after the Romans left Britain, and the raids of Saxon tribes began to be felt, the roads, which during the Roman times had been kept in good repair, were neglected. Some of them gradually dropped out of use, and in the course of time grass, brushwood, and trees grew close up to the track and in places covered it, and it became in time a "lost" road. The roads which remained in use, through neglect grew worse and worse, and all through the Middle Ages very little was done to mend them. Travellers for the most part journeyed on horseback, and trains of mules and pack-horses transported goods. Later on heavy wagons, drawn by teams of eight, ten, or a dozen horses were

used, and frequently extra teams had to be hitched on
at places where they got into difficulties and came
to grief owing to the badness of the road. Often these
long trains of wagons had to be "convoyed" by bands
of armed men on horseback. To repair "foul and
noyous highways" was regarded as a work of mercy,
and we often find good people in the Middle Ages
leaving money in their wills to be bestowed on the
repair of a part of a highway. The religious houses

Cart, Fourteenth Century
From an illuminated manuscript in the Bodleian Library, Oxford

in many cases were expected to keep up good roads in
their own neighbourhood. There was once a hermit,
who lived at Highgate, near London. He, at his own
cost, had gravel dug from the top of Highgate Hill,
and with it made a causeway down in the "hollow
way" between Highgate and Islington. In the fourteenth
century the Bishop of London made a way through his
park at Highgate Hill across Finchley Common to
Whetstone, near Barnet, because the highway was
in such a dreadful condition. Those who used this
road had to pay a toll.

After the dissolution of the monasteries the various
parishes were expected to look after the parts of the

great roads which ran through them, the landlords
and tenants being required, according to the size of
their holdings, to furnish men and horses, wagons
and barrows, to work on the highways for so many
days in each year. But for some centuries the work
was done in a very shiftless, casual manner. The people
in the parishes grumbled and did as little as they could,
for, as they said, it was not they who wore out the roads,
but the travellers from a distance who came backwards
and forwards with all their heavy loads.

Traffic increased as the time went on, and it became
necessary to provide for the wants of the many travellers
along the roads. The old villages in very many cases stood
away from the highways, and so we find new hamlets
springing up on the main roads, and some of the new
towns, like Uxbridge, Brentford, and Edgware in
Middlesex, and Buntingford in Hertfordshire, had their
origin in this way. Similar instance will be found in
most other counties.

In Queen Elizabeth's reign the roads all over the
country were bad; in some parts, owing to the nature
of the soil, particularly bad. In the south, in the Weald
district, the iron workers were ordered to mend their
roads with the cinders from their furnaces, as the stone
found in that neighbourhood was too soft for the purpose. But the roads did not greatly improve although
the amount of traffic upon them increased.

Coaches came into use for long-distance travelling in
the reign of Charles II. One began to run regularly
between London and Bath in 1667—a three-days' journey
if no accidents happened—and another started running
from London to Portsmouth in the following year. About
the middle of the eighteenth century every week there
passed through the Borough from London on the way
south, a hundred and forty-three stage-coaches, a hundred and twenty-one wagons, and a hundred and ninety-

six carts and caravans. That was only the out-going traffic, there was quite as much traffic returning to the City.

It was about the year 1754 that a great improvement of roads began through the passing of the Turnpike Acts. The idea was that those people who actually used the roads should bear the cost of their upkeep, and companies, or "trusts", were formed to look after certain roads, have them properly made, and kept in repair. At certain distances along the road, a few miles apart, gates were set across the road with a little house by each, in which the toll-gate keeper lived, whose duty it was to open and close the gate to travellers and take the specified toll. Different kinds of vehicles had to pay different sums as toll, and so had flocks of sheep and droves of cattle when being moved from one part of the country to another. People actually living in the neighbourhood had certain rights to use the way toll free. The toll-gate keeper was usually a "crusty" person—a sort of spider lying in wait to catch

A Toll-gate, early Nineteenth Century. From a contemporary painting

flies—and very often when a traveller drove up to the gate in a hurry, anxious to get through, the toll-man would be particularly slow in opening the gates and in giving change.

Most of the main roads were thus improved, but not all of them. As late as the year 1797 the turnpike road through Uxbridge, which carried a very large traffic, was very bad indeed. There was only one track which could be used in winter and that was eight inches deep in slush and mud. Still, on the whole, the roads were improving and coaches were able to travel more quickly.

Mail-coaches were put on the road in 1785, and they increased in speed and in numbers as the years went on, until just before the advent of railways. Over ninety coaches a day passed through Whetstone Turnpike, near Barnet; and in 1821 there were coaches which did the seventy-two miles between London and Portsmouth in ten hours. It was the same on all the great roads, and the coaches were only one part of the traffic.

In the "good old coaching days", noblemen and great folk travelled the long distances in their family coaches in great state, attended by servants; some riding before and after on horseback, and some hanging on behind the coach. Other wealthy people used to travel "post", and the carriages used were called "post-chaises". These were drawn by four or six horses, with a "post-boy" or postilion to each pair of horses. No matter how old he might be he was always called a post-boy. A great many old-established inns all over the country are still called "posting-houses". At these inns such carriages and horses to draw them, and post-boys to drive them, could be hired. These houses were about ten miles apart, and that distance was called a "stage"; and in posting the horses were changed at each "house" along the road. Nowadays, by the name posting-house we understand an inn where vehicles and

Coach, early Nineteenth Century

horses can be hired; but probably not one of them could turn out a post-chaise, four horses and a couple of post-boys, at five minutes' notice.

The railways gradually drove the coaches and the post-chaises off the roads, but the introduction of cycles in the last quarter of the nineteenth century, and the motor-car at the beginning of the twentieth century have revived the use of the highways for traffic, and there is a great time for the old roads just ahead of us to-day.

There were many varieties of inns, often quite close together, from the big posting-houses down to the obscure little ale-house. These houses accommodated various classes of traffic. Even now, if you live near to one of the big main roads you will notice that some wagons draw up at particular houses on the road for

THE NEW INN, GLOUCESTER

From an engraving published in 1830. This building is still in use

.

"refreshment of man and beast"—the hay-carts have
their own special stopping places, and so, too, have
other sorts of heavy traffic; and they have kept to
the custom of the road from one generation to another.
The old inns are often very picturesque buildings and
there are some famous ones in every county. The
curious names by which they are known is a study in
itself, and quite an interesting one.

Many of the old inns fell on evil days as the introduction of railways gradually absorbed most of the road
traffic, and many of them were closed or turned into
private houses. In the last quarter of the nineteenth
century life on the ancient highways began to revive
through the introduction of cycling as a means of loco-
motion. Cycling became very common, and, by
specially catering for cyclists a good number of these
old inns came again to prosperous times. With the
dawn of the twentieth century motor-cars came on the
road, and still further brought the highways into use.
But these raised "clouds of dust" and tore up the roads,
and it became a great problem how to make the roads
suitable for this new sort of traffic, and a good deal was
done which improved their surface greatly. Then came
the Great War, and a continuous stream of heavier
motor-traffic had to be put upon the roads throughout
the country to supply the huge camps at home and over-
seas, and the many new towns which have sprung up
in districts which, a few years ago, were quiet, un-
frequented places. There is an enormous amount of
work to be done now in re-making the present roads and
tracks, and to provide for many new ones as well. We
now realize that rapid means of transit for both people
and goods will have to be provided on a far larger scale
than we have hitherto attempted, if the resources of the
country are to be properly developed. Roads, more
roads, better roads are an urgent necessity.

CHAPTER XLIX

Roads—Railways

In speaking of the roads in the last chapter, we have come right down to the present day and its needs; but we must go back a bit, as far as time is concerned, to say something about one special class of road which has played an important part in the making of England. The story of the roads began before the dawn of written history—ages and ages before. The story of the railways belongs, as we may say, only to yesterday.

When we speak of a railway in these days we picture to our minds a trackway, laid with parallel steel rails, along which long trains of carriages and trucks are drawn by a locomotive engine. The engine, indeed, is the first thing that a boy thinks of in connection with a railway; and no wonder, for the "iron horse" is a marvellous and interesting piece of machinery. But in the history of our modern railways the *trackway*, or the *rail-way* proper, comes first. There were railways long before there were locomotive engines; indeed, we shall not be far out if we say that there were railways in England a few centuries before steam-engines of any sort came into use.

It was up in the North, in the colliery districts by the Tyne, that the idea of tramways, along which trains of trucks, drawn by horses or mules, seem to have first come into use; and they can certainly be traced there as far back as the time of King Charles I (about the year 1630). The first railway which Parliament allowed to be laid in the South of England was the "Surrey Iron Railway". This connected Croydon with Wandsworth, and, later on, it was extended to Merstham. That was about the year 1801, and was intended to convey mer-

George Stephenson's Locomotive " The Rocket", which at its trial trip in 1830 ran 29 miles an hour

chandise, not passengers. For a time it was of great service to mills and factories on the River Wandle. That was the first railway in that part of the country, and the trucks were drawn by donkeys!

A writer of that time, who thought that he was a very wise, far-seeing man, gave it as his opinion "that it was not probable that railways would ever come into general use!" Well, it is never very wise to prophesy until you really know.

Nearly every new invention has been scoffed at at first. Even in this present century, when the early experiments in the use of air-craft were being made, thousands of persons gravely shook their heads in disapproval, declaring that man was never intended to "fly". The Great War time has seen wonderful developments in air-craft, and so many "impossible" things have been achieved that we can realize, just a little bit, that air-craft has "a great future" before it, greater than we can as yet grasp.

It would be impossible to give here even a bare outline of the story of the English Railways, but the making of these railways and their use and development brought about rapidly many marvellous changes which have affected the life of the nation.

Seventy and eighty years ago, when railways were first being made, they excited a great deal more attention and interest than they do to-day. Railways were so new then, for one thing, and there were so many of them being made about the same time for another thing. There are hundreds of miles of railway going through quiet country districts, which were made many years ago, and there are thousands of people living in those districts who have been born since the railways were made. To them the railway is as much an everyday thing as the old parish church, the town pump, or the river. So far as *they* are concerned, the line has been always there—they never saw the country-side before the railway came. But in the years—say between 1830 and 1860—the work was watched with much interest, and it excited much talk, both wise and foolish.

What did the people who lived in a country village see? Long before the navvies came, for years in fact, the coming railway was talked about. The surveyor, with his attendants, carrying theodolite and measuring-chain, as he went about his work "taking levels", was very narrowly watched, and his sayings and doings were noted and discussed, time after time. In fact, not un-frequently the surveyor and his men had some very lively experiences, for there were lots of places in which they were regarded with suspicion, and all sorts of tricks were played upon them. Stephenson, when out survey-ing, was threatened with more than one ducking in a horse-pond; guns were fired at him, and he had to get through his work at all sorts of odd times. There was one surveyor who took a professional prize-fighter with him as his assistant, and he found work for him to do besides merely helping him in land-surveying. Bulls were sometimes turned loose in the fields in which surveyors were busy, and they had to leave in a hurry. Surveyors were quite used to meeting with all sorts of abuse, and being faced by angry men, armed with brickbats and pitchforks.

Then, when the road was staked out, and carts and men began to arrive, and a whole town of huts for the workers on the railway was set up on the broad hill-side, where the villagers and their fathers before them, time out of mind, had ploughed, and sowed, and harrowed, and reaped, and gleaned—tongues would wag still more, and curiosity would be intensified. When the huts were finished the navvies arrived. Strange folk they were to the villagers, speaking a language of their own, and living by themselves—strong, powerful men, doing great deeds of strength, capable of working hard, and very often of drinking hard, and of fighting hard. The quiet little inns and ale-houses became noisy and busy. The navvies brought change and excitement with them ; and also, at times, mischief, strife, confusion, and drunkenness. For miles round the farmers would complain that they could get no labour for farm-work. Young men, attracted by the novelty, the higher wages, and the greater numbers, turned navvies, "learned their works" and left the old agricultural life of their forefathers for ever. Then, when the navvies set to work, the villagers saw them busy, like ants upon the hill-side, cutting a great cleft through it, many feet in depth. As they came along, yard by yard, they saw a rough tramway laid, along which long trains of trucks, drawn by a noisy, fussy little engine, were being drawn, some full of earth and gravel or stone which had been cut away.

Building a Railway in the early Nineteenth Century

Then, after many months' work, the men advanced out on to the open plain. For weeks and months trains of trucks were constantly coming laden with earth, which was tipped on to the lower ground, forming an embankment, which gradually came nearer and nearer the river bank. Down by the river bank, on the far side, and on the near side as well, were men digging for weeks at a time. Then, these made way for an army of brick layers and masons, and loads and loads of brick and stone were brought along the line, or dragged by horses through the old country lanes to the waterside. There, on each side of the stream, what looked like big towers were erected, as tall as the church tower, or taller perhaps, and still the earth day by day was being brought along the way and tipped, adding to the embankment yard by yard. Such earth, too; clay, perhaps, or earth of such kind as the oldest man in the parish had never seen in those parts before, because it had been brought from a place or places many miles away.

Then, when the brickwork on each side of the river was in position, there was the building of a bridge to watch. There were several huge arches of brick, or perhaps of stone, brought from far-off quarries. But what were those queer, lattice-work things, looking something like spiders' webs, which were brought down to the waterside? There was nothing like that ever seen in the village before. What did it mean? They saw these great iron lattice-work sections hoisted in the air by steam cranes and swung slowly up and round till they were placed in position, resting on the piers of masonry. It must have been a wonderful sight to watch the river being spanned by a huge bridge or by these girders, and to see the different sections being fitted and fastened together.

You may be sure that there was much shaking of heads and many prophecies that this sort of thing was a flying in the face of Providence—just as in our own time there has been over cycles, motor-cars, and aircraft. How could those great trains and heavy engines pass safely over such a flimsy-looking bridge as that? It would be sure to snap in the middle. And when an accident happened—and sad accidents did happen—

Sankey Valley Viaduct, constructed by George Stephenson on the Liverpool and Manchester Railway (1826-9). After a contemporary painting. By permission of the London and North-Western Railway Company

many declared that it was the Almighty's judgment upon men for thinking that they knew better than their fathers before them.

So the work went on, and in time the railway became an accomplished fact and was no longer a wonder, and a race grew up to whom railways became part and parcel of everyday life.

But the railways brought many other changes. Those loads of earth brought from distant parts of the line not only altered the appearance of the country where they were deposited, but caused other alterations as well. Grass soon grew on the slopes of these embankments, but with the grass came up also strange weeds and plants. These seeded, the wind scattered the seeds, and, in the fields on either side of the line, these new weeds showed themselves the next season. For a year or two, probably, nobody noticed this very particularly; but, before very long, whole districts might be overrun with varieties of weeds never seen in that district before.

In some places marshes had to be drained, and, in consequence, many broad, shallow stretches of water disappeared. Such "sedgy pools" in quiet districts were once the haunt of many varieties of wild fowl. As the pools have disappeared the wild fowl which made these their haunt disappeared also, and with them the wild flowers and water-plants belonging thereto have died out as well. In much the same way insects have been imported in the loads of earth and found a home in a new district where they have, so to speak, "settled", and have done in some cases good, and in other cases harm, to the land.

Many cuttings through the beds of gravel and rocks have taught us something of the changes which have taken place in the earth's crust. It has been possible to examine the structure of the soil of many parts of England more thoroughly in the deep railway cuttings and tunnels than could have been done in any other way. Geologists have gathered much most valuable information from the soil and rock dug out in railway excavations.

*The Town Hall, Carlisle, built in time of Elizabeth.   From a drawing
made in 1780*

CHAPTER L

Government

There was not much change for many centuries in the
way in which towns and villages were governed.

The borough towns, which gained their charters back
in the days of King John, or King Henry III, had them
confirmed by various kings in later times; but the powers
of the towns were not much altered.   The corporation of
a borough was usually made up of men chosen by the
freemen; but, if the freemen did not admit many persons
to the freedom of the borough, the power of electing,
in the course of years, fell into the hands of a very few
people.

This was what actually happened in a very large

number of cases, and at the end of the eighteenth century there were many old boroughs which were governed by "close corporations"—the bulk of the people living in the borough having no voice in the management of the affairs of the town. All that was altered in the early part of the nineteenth century. Many of the old boroughs lost their privileges, as they had become such small unimportant places. All other boroughs now have regular elections of town councillors by the inhabitants each first of November. The councils elect the mayor on each 9th of November.

The mayor, and some of the inhabitants of the borough, are also magistrates and attend to police cases; while the town council looks after matters connected with sewers, lighting, paving, and cleansing the streets of the town. It has now also charge of educational affairs in many of the big towns, a committee of each county council being the educational authority in all other parts of the country.

In London and large towns, where there is much police court business, there are special magistrates, trained lawyers, who attend to nothing else.

In country places, for centuries, the manor court governed the manor; but gradually, and by Tudor times, most of the power of the manor court, or court leet as it was sometimes called, had passed into the hands of the Vestry. This consisted of the parish officers and rate-payers in the whole parish. It was called the vestry because its meeting-place was the vestry of the parish church, or even the church itself.

The relief of the poor and the care of the highways provided the vestry with most of its business. The churchwardens had special care of the property of the church, but in Tudor times they were also charged with the relief of the poor. To help them in this work two overseers, at least, in each parish, were chosen every

Police Officer and Jailer, early Nineteenth Century.
A scene from " Oliver Twist " (Charles Dickens)

year. All the rate-payers were liable to serve in turn if elected, unless they could show a good reason for not serving. The elections took place about Lady Day. The vestry fixed what rates were to be made, and the overseers col-lected them. But the overseers had to be admitted to their office, and all rates allowed, by two justices of the peace, before they were legal.

It became neces-sary, as the poor law business increased, to have constables to help the overseers in keeping an eye on strangers, vagrants and beggars who came into the parish. These, too, had to serve for one year. In big parishes they were assisted by a beadle, and had, with the help of all the inhabitants in turn, to keep watch and ward at night. Very unpleasant work they had to do in towns and places just outside towns. In London, and in many other towns also, to help the " watch " there were special officers called " watchmen ", whose duty it was to parade the streets at night at regular intervals, and " call the hour "—" Past two o'clock, and a frosty morning ". One of their duties was to arrest any dis-orderly characters whom they might come across on their rounds. But as each watchman carried a lighted lantern that, together with the noise he made, gave ample warning to that sort of people, who could usually, without much difficulty, get out of the watchman's way. When he did come upon the track of any of these gentry he would " sound his rattle " as a signal for the "watch" to come to his assistance, and, if they could, arrest the offenders. This duty of watching and warding had to be carried out until towards the middle of the nineteenth century, when our present system of police was established. Beadles and constables had to see to the whippings, which were so common, and to setting people in the stocks and the cage; to moving sick and diseased wretches on to the next parish, and other unpleasant duties.

The surveyors of the highways had to see that each person who was liable did his share of the work of the highways, or paid for having it done. But by far the most important business was that of the churchwardens and overseers. They had to settle in what houses the poor folk were to live, who were to look after them, what allowance was to be made for them. The poor usually had their money paid to them at church, monthly. Then the overseers had to see that every able-bodied man was at work, often having to provide the work, to place out apprentices, and to supply flax or wool for the women and children to spin. Sometimes the poor were boarded out; some of them lived in cottages, or in the poors' house which the parish built. Then, too, these officers had to relieve beggars, and persons passing through the parish.

This work of providing for the poor was very difficult and very anxious, especially at the end of the eighteenth and in the early part of the nineteenth century. It was quite a common practice for big parishes to "farm out" the care of the poor to the highest bidder. That is, a man would contract with the parish authorities to look after the relief of the poor in that parish for a certain sum of money per annum, for so many years.

Then poor law unions were formed, and union workhouses built, in which the helpless poor might be better cared for, and vagrants and wanderers find a night's lodging. These were looked after by Boards of Guardians, especially elected for that purpose. We have not a perfect plan yet, by any means, but much care and thought is being given to this question, and many changes, which we hope will be improvements in the administration of the Poor Law, are being taken in hand. The difficulties of how to deal with the poor who, through no fault of their own, cannot help themselves, and how to deal with those who are lazy and will not work, are very great.

The work of the old vestries has now passed to the parish councils, the district councils, and the county councils. The work is important, and has much to do with the welfare of our towns and villages. We must not expect that these bodies can do everything at once, or that they will make no mistakes. More people now than ever have a direct voice in the work of these various councils, and it is the duty of everyone to take a real interest in their work, and to strive to improve it in every possible way. If we know something of the past history of our towns and villages it will help us to form a right judgment concerning difficulties which have to be met in the present, and so to act that those who come after us may be able to go on building upon our work, that there may be nothing to undo, nothing to blame, but that future years may say of our times:—

" They knew how to work, and they worked on right principles." " Do justly, love mercy, walk humbly."

CHAPTER LI

Some Changes

There was not much alteration in the outward appearance of the villages and the " look " of the country round them for many centuries. Indeed even now many of the villages themselves are not greatly altered in their general arrangement. Down to the times of the Tudor kings the old land and manor customs had gone on since Saxon days, changing but very slowly. Many of the class which had been villeins in the Middle Ages had become yeomen; some had got lands of their own, and some land on the old manors, which they rented. But they did not alter very much the old way of treating the land, and it was only gradually that farm-houses sprang up away from the villages.

In some parts of the country these lonely farm-houses are more common than in others. There are, for instance, a good many in the Weald of Sussex which sprang up first as huts in forest clearings, and afterwards became houses with farm-buildings attached to them.

On the borders of great lonely heaths and commons we can often see very old and very small cottages, with walls of clay, or wood, or stone, according to the district in which they happen to be. Long ago some squatter built his little hut here, and out of pity, perhaps, or through carelessness, the lord of the manor took no notice. There he remained, year after year, until custom allowed him to look upon it as his own; and in time it actually became his private property. Such squatters in lonely places were often looked upon more or less with fear by the timid folk living in the distant village. They did not care to do or say anything to upset the stranger, fearing for the safety of their sheep, cattle, and poultry.

Many little holdings and small farms began in this way.

Many of the farms, though they were separate holdings, still had strips in the big fields of the parish. The crops were sown and gathered according to the ancient customs, and the cattle turned into them and out on the waste lands at certain seasons, just as they had been in the Middle Ages.

But about the beginning of the eighteenth century there was a pretty general movement towards breaking up these big fields into separate parts, and letting each farmer have his portion to himself, so that he might know exactly what land was his and what belonged to his neighbour. So it came to pass that Enclosure Acts were passed for parish after parish. The old common arable fields were divided among those who had rights in them. Then many of the old wastes, heaths, commons, and marshes were treated in the same way.

That caused a great change in the appearance of the parish. Instead of the fields in long, straight strips, with unploughed balks between them, the strips belonging to each farmer were thrown into one, and hedgerows planted. In time they became smooth fields, separated from each other by hedges, in which grew here and there timber trees. The old cart-tracks, winding across and round the common fields, in time became lanes bounded by high hedges. The trackways across many of the old wastes and commons in a similar way were turned into lanes, and the waste broken up into fields. Still, a good deal of the waste land was left, and has never yet been enclosed. So far as we can see now, this is not likely to happen, because we feel more and more every year that, for the sake of the health and recreation of the people, it is absolutely necessary to preserve as many open spaces as possible. Some of these wastes and uncultivated, or only partially cultivated, lands

Hayes Barton Farm, Devonshire, the reputed birthplace of Sir Walter Raleigh (1552). It is in the picturesque Elizabethan style, with thatched and gabled roof, mullioned windows, and gabled porch

have been brought under the spade and the plough during the war-time, and all over the country people have heartily set to work to increase our "home-grown" food supply.

The fields, the hedgerows, and the lanes which delight us so much in the country are, most of them, some two hundred years old.

When the farm had its own separate fields allotted to it, it became convenient for the farmer to live in the midst of his land. So we find the farm-house and its buildings, with a few labourers' cottages, a long way out of the village, and away from the church. If you take notice you will find that from this outlying farm-house there is usually a pretty straight field-path to the parish church.

A good deal could be said about our forests and wood-lands—their importance, and the part they have played in the making of England. In the seventeenth and eighteenth centuries especially, there was great attention paid to the cultivation of trees, and many of the owners of private park-lands did excellent work in promoting the growth of timber. But in the nineteenth century there seems to have been a considerable falling-off in this respect, and far-seeing men at times warned us that we needed to pay more attention to trees and forests and to the growth of timber. The terrible blizzard which swept over the country in March, 1916, brought down thousands and thousands of fine old trees, and the needs of our army and navy during the war-time has made sad havoc in parks and plantations, so that one of the urgent needs of the days in front of us is systematic attention to " afforestation ", in order to " make good " the terrible wastage.

Hamlets have grown up away from the old village green, its church, and its manor-house. The roads were often so bad that horses frequently cast their shoes, tires came off wheels, and wheels came off carts and coaches ; so under many " a spreading chestnut-tree " a little smithy and wheel-wright's shop arose. A smithy is always a centre of life and news, as everybody knows. You can see to-day, along many of our roads, sheds and shops being opened, where broken-down cycles and motor-cars can be repaired and supplied with odds and ends which they may happen to need. Round these hamlets have in time sprung up, and in scores of places the hamlet has become of more importance than the old village, and has grown into a little town, with new churches and chapels and public buildings.

In these war-years large numbers of quite new town-ships of enormous size have sprung up in connection with the making of munitions, and the provision of hospitals and camps, and as yet we know very little about them as a whole. Some are only temporary, but others have "come to stay", and in them new industries on a big scale will probably be developed. All this means change—change of appearance, change of ideas, change of methods.

Then there are the districts where new industries and manufactures have been planted. That is too large a subject to deal with here, but think of the great changes these have wrought on the face of the country in the coal and mineral districts of England in the last two hundred years!

Again, there are the railways. Notice how little townships have grown up round the railway stations, especially on the main lines in districts near a big town. Houses spring up for the hosts of people who, like streams of human ants, hurry to the station to catch the early morning trains, and, as the afternoon wears into evening, come again from the station to snatch a few hours' rest at home.

We have said nothing of

"The beauty and mystery of ships,
And the magic of the sea",

and the part they have had in the making of our towns and villages. This subject would require not only one but many books, and then we shall only just have begun to think about it, and to find out how little we know. Our wonderful Navy, our Merchant Sailors, our Fishermen—what do we *not* owe to them for what they have done for us in the terribly anxious times through which we have passed and are still passing! It is good, in spite of all the awful suffering, to have lived through these years, and to have seen something of what can be done by sacrifice of self, co-operation, and just "sticking to duty"—on land, on sea, under the sea, and in the air, in busy towns, and in quiet country places.

Yes, the life of our towns and villages is a very interesting subject. Nature and Man each works for and with the other; both are full of mystery, life, beauty, and high inspiration, if we could only use our eyes to see, our intelligence to understand, our hearts to sympathize, and our hands to work, for the things that are true, and lovely, and pure.

TEST QUESTIONS

CHAPTER I.—Where is Canada? What is meant by the backwoods?

Explain as well as you can why towns grow up in particular localities.

CHAPTER II.—Give examples of the remains that tell us of the existence of men in Britain in very olden times.

What are the earliest of these weapons and implements called in museum catalogues? How were they made?

CHAPTER III.—Who followed the Cave-dwellers or River-driftmen in the occupation of Britain?

Discuss the following stages of development: the hunting stage; the pastoral stage; the agricultural stage.

Describe the huts of the Pit-dwellers; state where they are found.

How did the Lake-dwellers prepare their habitations?

CHAPTER IV.—What is meant by a barrow? What kinds of barrows exist in Britain?

What is supposed to have been the use of stone circles? Name the best known of these in Britain.

Give an account of how the circle at Stonehenge is supposed to have been formed.

Make out a list of the stone circles you have heard of and tell what you know about them.

CHAPTER V.—Tell what you know of the reasons for the invasion of Britain by the Romans.

Explain how Roman roads are laid bare and describe their character.

Explain why "oyster shells" should often be met with in quantities at places far distant from the river mouths.

Where must the great body of the Britons have lived in Roman times?

Who attacked Britain when the Romans withdrew?

Why was the attack by the Scots from Ireland and the north so hard on the Britons?

What proofs have we that Christianity was introduced into Britain during Roman times?

When did the English, or, as they were called, the Saxons, first invade Roman Britain?

CHAPTER VI.—State as clearly as you can how the English (Saxons) came to Britain.

Explain why the English did not care for walled towns.

The British were largely hunters and shepherds and the English farmers and fishermen; what changes took place in the country on the English settling in it?

What happened to the Britons?

From what languages are the names of most English rivers and hills derived?

In what part of Britain were the first English settlements made?

CHAPTER VII.—Explain how English village communities were governed.

Draw from memory a plan of an English village settlement.

How were the strips to be allotted to each villager fixed?

What was the village folk-moot?

CHAPTER VIII.—Explain how the English fixed on the position for their "tun" or village.

Why did the villagers build their houses near each other?

Describe as clearly as you can the village of "Exton" in Rutlandshire.

Account for the resemblance of one English country town to another.

How and by whom was the land of the village divided?

What other land besides the arable land belonged to the village?

CHAPTER IX.—Explain what was meant by *tything* and by *hundred* and show what place they took in old English government.

Account for the varied number of *hundreds* into which English shires are divided.

Tell what you know about the old English kingdoms, their fight for power, and the results the struggle had.

Why was the country divided into shires? Who was placed at the head of the shire?

How were the various shires or shares into which the country was divided named?

CHAPTER X.—Account for the gradual growth of trade among communities such as those which first settled in England.

Where did the English towns grow up? Why?

Give examples of English towns built on sites of Roman towns.

Why did the people build walls round their towns?

Explain why towns were more inclined to hold out against their overlords than villages were.

How was it that the king came to be the protector of the towns?

CHAPTER XI.—With what did the early English dioceses correspond? Give reasons for this.

Explain the steps by which Christianity spread through England.

Who appointed the village priest, and how was he maintained?

What are monasteries? Give an account of their establishment in England.

Explain how life in a monastery or convent differed from life in a "tun" or village.

Explain the reason for what are known as market crosses.

CHAPTER XII.—Explain the sort of life led by the early monks.

What effect had these lives of toil and usefulness on the lives of the laymen of the time?

Explain how "vills" came into the hands of the monks.

Give an example of the great gifts bestowed by king and nobles on monasteries.

What kind of "lords" did the abbots make for towns?

Why should we expect the monks to have been, on the whole, better masters than the lay lords?

From whom is it that accounts of these times have come down to us? What do you infer?

Account for the growth of the possessions of the monasteries.

How did the monasteries draw to themselves skilled workers?

Show that the Danish invasions helped to bring England into closer contact with the Continent.

CHAPTER XIII.—Explain what a typical English village was like at the beginning of the eleventh century.

Who were the *geburs* and the *cottiers*? Explain the difference.

Distinguish between *socmen* and *villeins*, or geburs and cottiers.

Who formed the *slaves* or *theows* of the period, and how were they treated?

What position did the *steward* or *reeve* hold?

Explain how the work of the tun was done, and how the villagers rewarded the smith, the carpenter, and the mason.

Give an account of the origin of trades unions or guilds.

Explain the principle on which the land of the village was cultivated.

How was the land divided among the villagers?

What rights had the villeins in the rough commons or forests?

For what purposes were the courts or meetings held?

Why did the towns claim and cling to self-government?

CHAPTER XIV.—Why was land in the eleventh century set apart for the uses of the Church?

Distinguish between parish churches and cathedral churches.

Explain why lands were left to monasteries and other religious institutions, and what the founders expected in return.

How were religious houses used during the Danish invasions?

Tell a story showing how people tried to put the Danes off the scent of their wealth.

Discuss, from the point of view of the monks and those who had sought shelter in the monastery, the action of the man who pretended to send his wealth there.

Explain how the king came to be regarded as the owner of the grazing and forest lands known as commons.

Describe the ways in which the monks helped England to improve.

CHAPTER XV.—Discuss the buildings before the Conquest that have been preserved for us.

What do the bits of sculpture forming the doorways tell us?

Describe an English house before the Conquest.

In monasteries what formed the centre of the group of buildings; and of what did these consist?

Explain why stone was introduced for building.

What were the arrangements for cooking?

Where and how were meals served?   What does lord mean?

CHAPTER XVI.—What did William of Normandy do with the lands that had belonged to Harold and his followers?

How did William treat the English nobles and thanes?

What were they compelled to do?

How, while making great grants of lands to his Norman followers, did William weaken their comparative power?

What became of the lands held by the Church?

Tell the story of Abbot Frederick of St. Albans.

How did William make sure that the monks would support him?

CHAPTER XVII.—What were the conditions on which the Conqueror granted lands to English earls and thanes?

Under the Norman system, who was supposed to be the owner of all the land in the country?

What were the tenants who held their lands direct from the king called (*tenants-in-chief*)?   Describe the method of swearing allegiance.

How did these tenants deal with the lands they held?

Describe the way an army was called together in feudal times.

If a lord had several manors, how were those on which he did not live managed?

What is the great record of the land of England, of its owners, of the character of the stock on it, &c., drawn up in William's reign, called?

CHAPTER XVIII.—Explain why the coming of the Normans to England should have introduced a period of great building activity.

What were the forms in which the rage for building shown at this time expressed itself?

Where can specimens of Norman work be seen still?

What was the character of Norman work at the beginning?

How did its character change?

CHAPTER XIX.—Explain why people built castles in different parts of the country.

What was their object in selecting particular sites for these erections?

Name some of the important castles you know, and describe the ruin you know best.

Explain why we so often find a castle or its ruins near a city or town.

CHAPTER XX.—Explain how a castle protected and controlled the district.

What did the numerous castles built during Stephen's reign become?

Give an account of the sufferings of the common people in Stephen's time.

Explain why Henry II destroyed such a large number of castles.

What were the Crusades, and when did they begin?

Show how the towns benefited from the wish of their lords to join the Crusades.

What had the baron or bishop to give the town as an equivalent for the money it lent?

CHAPTER XXI.—Why were so many monasteries built after the Conquest?

Give an account of the causes that had led to a weakened interest in Church affairs in England.

How were the religious houses in Normandy superior to those in England?

What is meant by an order of monks?

How were the English monasteries reformed? Name some of the more important of these.

How did the people feel with regard to alien priories?

What did Edward I do with regard to these?

The monasteries also held lands. How did they manage them?

Where were the monasteries situated?

What other work besides farming was carried on by the monks?

To what extent did the monasteries undertake the education of the people?

Explain how the monks were the book-producers of the time.

What did they do to improve the English trade in wool?

CHAPTER XXII.—Explain what differences would seem most striking in passing from a modern manufacturing town to an old town or village.

Describe the gradual decay of old houses in a town.

Why do people regret the passing away of these old houses?

How far back do some still existing old houses date?

Tell what you know about "The Jew's House", Lincoln.

Of what material were most houses built in early times?

Of what are most houses both in town and country now built?

What is the oldest brick house in England?   How old is it?

When was brick-making first generally used in England after the time of the Romans?

Discuss the loss of the art of brick-making after the withdrawal of the Romans.

CHAPTER XXIII.—What in reality were the houses of the earls and thanes copies of?

What was the most important part of the house?

Explain why it was found necessary to add other buildings to the hall.

Describe the house or hut of a villein.

What was meant by a "bay"?

Explain how it comes about that some of the old houses in villages stand on foundations dating back to before the Conquest.

What is the advantage of preserving some specimens of these old houses?

Explain why the houses must be improved.

Put the description of a countryman's house in your own words.

CHAPTER XXIV.—Explain why houses in towns have more frequently been altered and rebuilt than houses in villages.

What was the usual arrangement of the dwelling-house through all these centuries?

Where was the workshop?   What was under it, and what above it?

What part of the house was turned to the street?

Where was the cellar and how was it built?

Of what were the walls of the house above the cellar built?

What proofs have we that the Normans were careless builders?

How were the houses of the period furnished?

What was the condition of the poor in those times?

For what offence were they frequently punished?

How were strangers treated?

CHAPTER XXV.—How did public health suffer in those times?

Who took the lead in developing drainage schemes?

What has been found out to be the purpose of the underground passages met with near the ruins of old monasteries?

How were the chief streets paved?

What towns in those times were best drained?

How were the various trades distributed throughout the town?

What was the character of the streets?

Describe an Englishman's imaginary walk through his native town after his return from the wars in France in the time of Edward III.

How was the refuse in the streets a danger to health?

What was one of the most loathsome diseases of the time?

How were the lepers treated?

Give an account of the origin of hospitals in mediæval times.

Compare the methods of charity then and now.

CHAPTER XXVI.—Give an account of the origin of corporations.

How did the towns or village communities come under the power of the nobles?

What effect had the Norman Conquest on the trade of England?

What were the effects of the introduction into England of foreign workmen after the Conquest?

What did the charters granted to towns by kings and nobles give them?

What did the townsmen aim at?

Who were the overlords in those times?

Explain the difference between Borough Sessions and Petty Sessions.

What is meant by the Court of Quarter Sessions?

What are the Assizes? How often are they held?

When the Assizes are held, what must the sheriff of the county do?

Of what former ceremony is this the survival?

CHAPTER XXVII.—Explain how the land of the country was supposed to be shared out in Norman times.

State what you know about manors and parishes.

From what part of the parish did the king create new manors?

Where did the people of the new manors go to worship?

Explain how new parishes grew up.

What were parks in old England?

What was meant by empaling or impaling a park?

.What did the "enclosure" of these parks take from the villeins?

Explain how the complex system of land laws grew up.

Where were the records kept in olden times? Where now?

CHAPTER XXVIII.—Why is the church in most villages the oldest building in the village?

Tell the story of the visit of holiday-makers to an old church, and show how their pleasure might have been increased.

Explain, with the help of p. 94, the different forms of architecture that may be met with in an old parish church.

Give a list of the different periods of mediæval architecture, and state when each was used.

What do we learn from the effigies of Crusaders in old churches?

To what time do the cover-stones or incised slabs belong?

What are brasses; and what do they tell us?

CHAPTER XXIX.—Explain what happened to the church buildings in the fourteenth and fifteenth centuries.

Where are the most beautiful spires met with?

Describe a fourteenth-century tomb.

What effect had the great plague, the Black Death, on the English buildings of the time?

What credit is due to the wealthy wool-merchants of Edward III's time?

What did the guildsmen of the fourteenth and fifteenth centuries do for the parish churches?

How were churchwardens appointed? To whom were they responsible?

What formed the subjects for inquiry when the bishop or his representative visited the parish?

CHAPTER XXX.—Explain why changes took place more slowly in those old times than they do now.

What was the estimated population of England at the Conquest, and what is it supposed to have been at the end of the fifteenth century?

Discuss the effect of the Black Death on the population.

Where did the bulk of the population live?

How was the population divided?

What did the term "clergy" mean in the Middle Ages?

How did the two sets of courts, the civil courts and church courts, spring up?

Compare the laws that guided these courts.

Explain what was meant by claiming "benefit of clergy".

Show what abuses crept in.

What was the real cause of the struggle between Henry II and Thomas à Becket?

Show what benefit the villeins and serfs got from the Church.

Why were clerks employed by the kings and nobles of the time?

CHAPTER XXXI.—Tell what you know about fairs and their uses.

Explain why fairs were an absolute necessity in old times.

These fairs could only be held under grant or charter, and were considered as a privilege. Why was this so?

Give a list of big towns at which fairs are held.

What was the village "wake"? How did it lead to the "fair"?

To whom had outsiders to pay toll?

What happened to the shops in the village when the fair was being held?

How long did the fairs usually last?

How was the privilege got of attending a fair without paying toll?

How were fairs a cause of ill-feeling between the towns and the monasteries?

CHAPTER XXXII.—Explain why the village or town market-place is usually an interesting sight.

What is meant by a covered market?

Where formerly were cattle-markets usually held?

When and where are corn-markets usually held?

What sort of building is the market-house in most cases?

Where did the town council generally meet?

How do the different trades group themselves in the market?

What has happened to the market-cross in many cases?

What kind of business was done at the cross?

Make out a list of the instruments used for the punishment of offenders.

Distinguish between the uses of fairs and markets in the Middle Ages.

For what are market tolls now used?

What were market stall-holders formerly?

How in some cases is intimation of the opening and closing of the market made?

When can goods be sold in the market?

What is the business of the market officials appointed by the corporation?

CHAPTER XXXIII.—Name some of the more famous of the old English schools.

What language was taught in mediæval schools?

For whom were the monastery schools intended?

At what age did boys in the Middle Ages begin school?

Explain the character of school work in those times and give the reason for it.

Give an account of the training of a choir-boy in the Middle Ages.

How did the parish priest and parish clerk deal with the boys who helped them?

How did the boys get holidays in those times?

What were the boys of St. Alban's forbidden to do in 1310? Explain why they were forbidden.

What were " miracles " or " mysteries "?

What mishap befell Geoffrey de Gorham (died 1146), Abbot of St. Alban's?

What provision was made in the Middle Ages for poor scholars?

Tell what you know of William of Wykeham.

CHAPTER XXXIV.—Explain as well as you can how and when universities began in Western Europe.

Explain how scholars were encouraged to go to a university.

What happened at Oxford in King John's reign (1209)?

How many scholars appear to have been attending Oxford at the time?

Give an account of the foundation of hostels in the thirteenth century?

What order of monks settled at Oxford early in the thirteenth century?

What did they do for the university?

When did Walter de Merton establish the first of the Oxford colleges?

What was the special work of these new colleges?

When was the first college established at Cambridge?

Oxford and Cambridge are cities of colleges.   Give a list of some of the more important colleges in each of these universities and tell what you know about them.

Why was it likely that Oxford in the reign of Edward III would become the most famous of European universities?

Give a list of the newer universities in England.

Discuss the reasons for these universities being established where they are.

CHAPTER XXXV.—What dreadful disaster befell the country in the middle of the fourteenth century?

What proportion of the people are said to have been carried off by the Black Death?

What effect had the plague on the architecture of the time?

Discuss the meaning of manor, and show how rights in it were acquired.

How were rights in parts of the land of the manor leased out by the lords of the manor?

Instead of service, what did the villeins or cottiers in country districts give?

How was this equivalent paid at first?

How did this class of labourer come into existence?

What happened to the labourer if he left his lord's employment?

Under what conditions did he become free?

What effect had the Black Death on the condition of the labourer?

What were the objects of the laws passed at this time?

How did the "lords" try to meet the difficulties arising from the scarcity of labour?

How was the difficulty of the scattered bits of land belonging to the lord met?

When were some of the oldest of our existing farmhouses built?

CHAPTER XXXVI.—Discuss the chief industries of England in the fourteenth, fifteenth, and sixteenth centuries.

By whom were woollen manufactures introduced into England?

Why had the English wool manufacturers an advantage over the Continental?

After the Black Death what happened to the cloth trade?

What styles of architecture were in use at the end of the fourteenth and the beginning of the fifteenth centuries?

Where are the finest examples of these styles to be met with?

What conclusion may we come to with regard to these places?

What work did the trade guilds in these times perform?

What was their relation to the town or village?

How were the town corporations formed?

CHAPTER XXXVII.—Discuss the attitude of the Church towards the poor.

. What was the object with which many of the religious houses were founded?

What were the religious houses to the pilgrims in the Middle Ages?

How were pretended pilgrims detected?

Give some account of the laws by which society sought to put down beggars in the Middle Ages.

How many hospitals and lazar-houses were there in the city of London in 1536?

Which of these were saved by the city at the dissolution of religious houses?

What scheme for the poor did Bishop Ridley put forward?

What Acts dealing with beggars were passed after the Reformation in England?

What difficulty in dealing with the poor did the country after the Reformation have to face?

When were the severe laws against vagabonds passed?

Who were included under the term? (Proctors without Queen's authority, physiognomists, palmists, &c., fencers, bearwards, players, and minstrels.)

Give an account of the way work was provided in the different parishes.

What means were taken to keep down the number of poor in the parish?

Who were the officers chosen to look after the poor of the parish?

What part did the stocks and whipping-post play?

What duties were thrown upon each parish?

What court settled the disputes between parishes?

CHAPTER XXXVIII. —Explain the changes that took place in the castles and their arrangements in Edward III's time.

Describe some of the more important buildings erected in the fourteenth century.

What made the end of the fourteenth and the whole of the fifteenth century such a stirring time in England?

What effect had the Wars of the Roses on the power of the barons?

Explain how this happened.

From what class did the new nobility created by Henry VII spring?

Tell what you know about the " Kingmaker ".

Give an account of the defeat of Richard III at Bosworth Field.

How did Henry VII put down maintenance or the keeping of hosts of needless servants?

Give an account of how the king treated the Earl of Oxford.

Tell what you know about the position of nobles in Tudor times.

How did the sort of houses they built show the change?

CHAPTER XXXIX.—Explain why towns were more picturesque in Tudor times than they are now.

Economically, what was the great drawback to the multiplication of religious houses?

Describe as well as you can a town at the end of the fifteenth century.

Why is it absurd to speak of shutting the monasteries as throwing the people out of work?

What other purposes besides the religious did the monasteries serve?

How did the people who got the lands of the monasteries use them?

How were the poor treated by the new owners?

Why was sheep-farming extended after the Reformation?

Account for the agricultural stagnation during the Lancastrian and Yorkist period.

How did the new owners deal with the buildings connected with the religious bodies?

CHAPTER XL.—What became of the buildings of many of the former religious houses during the reign of Elizabeth?

Account for the building activity during the reign of Elizabeth, and for the introduction of Elizabethan architecture.

Describe the plan of an ordinary Elizabethan house.

Explain how it was built.

Where are these old Elizabethan houses found?

What effect have they on village scenery?

CHAPTER XLI.—Of what materials are the old Elizabethan houses built?

Name some of the most famous Elizabethan houses.

Describe the general plan of such houses.

When was the use of bricks for building introduced into England?

By whom were the mouldings for these buildings made?

Tell what you know about Inigo Jones and Jacobean architecture.

Explain the effect of the Great Fire of London on architecture.

CHAPTER XLII.—Why were the churches at the Reformation stripped of their ornaments?

What was done to those who did not attend the parish church after the Reformation?

What would have been done to them before the Reformation, and what was done to them in Roman Catholic countries after the Reformation?

Why were there secret chambers in old Elizabethan houses?

What new kind of monument was erected in the churches at this time?

For what purpose were some of the old chapels set apart at this time?

CHAPTER XLIII.—Who was Sir Christopher Wren?

Name some of the buildings he designed.

What changes in the design of houses marked the eighteenth century?

Why had Wren such an opportunity for showing his powers?

What part of the house received special attention as the eighteenth century proceeded?

Describe a doorway of the time.

What parts of the house were neglected?

What essentials of a comfortable house have still to be seen to?

CHAPTER XLIV.—Why were sermons thought so important after the Reformation?

What were the reasons for making the divisions between pews in churches so high?

What changes were introduced later for comfort?

How did the little girl describe a pew?

What reasons were there for more money being spent on churches in the Middle Ages than after the Reformation?

Why was money not as freely spent on churches in the seventeenth century as on houses?

When was bell-ringing introduced?

How did the monuments set up in Charles II's time differ from the earlier monuments?

To what time do the earliest grave-stones existing belong?

What do you know about Grinling Gibbons?

What was the character of the later seventeenth and early nineteenth century churches? Describe one.

What were the vaults under the church used for?

When were cemeteries introduced?

CHAPTER XLV. — Explain how some of the property of the religious houses was used for education after the Reformation.

Give an account of the origin of some of the grammar-schools after the Reformation.

It is estimated that there were in England prior to the Reformation over 200 grammar-schools. Name some of these still existing.

Give an account of the school founded at Norwich in 1632.

What were charity schools? When did they come into existence?

What was taught in these schools?

What do you know about the Blue-coat School? Describe the dress.

How was the charity schoolboy dressed?

On what lines were the parish schools formed?

Tell what you know of the educational work of Andrew Bell and Joseph Lancaster.

Tell what you know of the " British and Foreign School Society ", and of the " National Society ".

Give some account of the progress of education since 1870.

CHAPTER XLVI.—In the Middle Ages, how were boys and girls set to work?

What justification was there for this way of treating the young?

Explain how apprentices were treated in the seventeenth century, and what powers over them the master had.

What was the result of the apprenticeship system?

To what kind of trades were the children of the poor apprenticed?

CHAPTER XLVII.—Show how fond children are of play.

How far back do many of our English games go?

Give an account of a game at marbles.

State the games that are played in your neighbourhood, and the seasons when they are played.

Give as full a description as you can of the way of playing one of them.

Tell what you know of the history of tennis or " fives ".

When did football become popular?

CHAPTER XLVIII.—Give the reasons, historical and other, for all roads leading to London.

Distinguish between main roads and cross roads, and explain the uses of each.

What happened to the roads after the Romans left Britain?

How did people travel in the Middle Ages?

For what purposes did people in the Middle Ages often leave money?

Why were the religious houses expected to keep up the roads in their neighbourhood?

To whom was the duty entrusted after the Reformation?

What was the state of the roads in Elizabeth's time?

When did coaches begin to be used?

Give an account of the establishment of toll-gates and the passing of the Turnpike Acts.

Give examples to show how rapidly coaching increased in the last part of the eighteenth and first part of the nineteenth centuries.

What is meant by a posting-house?

What took the place of the coaches and road traffic?

What partial revival of the old inns took place in the latter half of the nineteenth century?

How do the railways now seem threatened?

CHAPTER XLIX.—Explain what is meant by a railway and show how this differs from older ideas.

How far back can trackways or railways be traced?

Give an account of the survey of a new line in the forties of last century.

Describe the way a railway was built and how the rustics who saw it gaped.

What science was greatly advanced by the making of railways?

CHAPTER L.—When did many English borough towns gain their charters?

How were the members of the Corporation chosen?

Of what did the Vestry consist? What was the duty of the churchwardens?

When were constables and beadles appointed? Who were the "watchmen"?

How did poor law unions come to be formed?

What bodies now do the work of the old vestries?

CHAPTER LI.—Explain the way farm-houses grew up away from villages.

Why were the villages afraid of the squatters?

When did the big fields of the three-shift system begin to be broken up?

What have the effects of the War been on our commons?

Explain what took place necessarily with the breaking up of the big field, or the enclosure of the commons.

Explain why the planting of trees has become so necessary.

Give an account of the growth of English hamlets away from the old villages.

Explain why new places grew up near railway stations in the neighbourhood of big towns.

What did our navy do for us during the Great War?

What did we owe to our merchant sailors and to our fishermen?